PRAISE FOR
THE PANIC ROOM

I love all things Troy Maxwell—his passion, vision and huge heart. However over the years I have admired his tenacious leadership. Troy's story is that of overcoming challenges and leading others to do so. *The Panic Room* will take you on that journey and infuse you with courage to overcome and live the life of an overcomer.

—*Sam Chand, Leadership Consultant and author of*
Leadership Pain *(www.samchand.com)*

Pastors Troy and Penny Maxwell have become incredibly dear friends of ours. They are extraordinary leaders, ministers, pastors and people. Their church, Freedom House, is one of the great churches in our generation. From the outside you would have no clue that Pastor Troy has been struggling with panic attacks and deep anxiety, which has become a pandemic in our generation. In this book Pastor Troy pulls back the curtains on this issue and the deep struggles that surround it, showing you how you can not only cope but, even more so, overcome!

—*Jurgen & Leanne Matthesius*
Awaken Church, San Diego

Too often, we only see or hear about a leader's best day. This creates an unrealistic view of their life. However, Troy gives us a glimpse of his worse day, the raw moment where he is feeling overwhelmed. The takeaways are incredible. They provide a pathway for handling difficult times. *The Panic Room* is a must read! Troy Maxwell has given us a map that journals a one-day-at-a-time miracle and guides us through the shadows of despair, dark lonely nights of fear, and the intimidating mountains of insecurities to climb. Like a trusted guide and confidante, Troy will help you walk through and win the attacks of anxiety and panic. You'll experience raw vulnerability from one of the most successful pastors in our generation and taste the sweet victory of Troy's ongoing journey. This book is your map to a miracle. As one of the charter members of Champions Network of Churches with Joel Osteen/Lakewood Church, Joel and I have often spoken about the character and life-giving ministry of Troy Maxwell. A man of grit and integrity, passion and compassion, I count Troy as a dear friend who has my highest admiration and respect.

—*Phil Munsey*
Chairman of Champions Network of Churches with
Joel Osteen/Lakewood Church

I am forever amazed at the genius of God to use humanity for His purpose and glory, when I fathom how flawed His children are at times. The trophies God often places in key positions can be far from perfect. In his book, *The Panic Room*, Troy Maxwell shares his gripping story of how living with panic attacks nearly destroyed his life and ministry, but the story doesn't end there because God's amazing grace brought restoration and renewal. If your life is being turned upside down due to some crisis right now, I highly recommend this book. What God did for Troy, He can do for you.

—*Marcus D. Lamb*
Founder and President
Daystar Television Network

I've watched Pastor Troy firsthand overcome his bouts with severe panic. This battle-proven memoir is packed with vulnerability and strength. His story is one that will lead many to sustained healing and enduring peace.

—*Marcus Mecum*
Senior Pastor
7 Hills Church

Troy's raw and authentic life story will move anyone who battles with one of the biggest issues facing our world today. This book is for anyone who has the courage to face their own personal "Panic Room".

—*Luke Barnett*
Senior Pastor, Dream City Church

Troy Maxwell knows that the key to being fearless is surrendering our worries to God. With candor, honesty and wisdom, *The Panic Room* reveals Troy's battle with fear and anxiety and, more importantly, his discovery of God's presence, power and purpose in the midst of it. This book is a must-read for anyone seeking the peace that passes understanding in the midst of life's overwhelming demands.

—*Chris Hodges*
Senior Pastor, Church of the Highlands
Author of The Daniel Dilemma *and* What's Next?

Too often we only see or hear, about a leader's best day; this creates an unrealistic view of their life. However, Troy Maxwell gives us a glimpse of his worse day, the raw moment where he is feeling his most overwhelmed. The takeaways are incredible, they provide a pathway for handling difficult times. The Panic Room is a must read.

—*Gerald Brooks, D.D., D.C.L.*

The Panic Room is a life-changing resource for anyone fighting the battle of anxiety and depression. In a world where many don't feel safe to be honest about their struggles, my friend Troy gives readers a raw, honest and vulnerable look at his own journey to freedom. I believe this book will encourage everyone who reads it and will light a path toward personal freedom.

—*Randy Bezet*
Lead Pastor, Bayside Community Church

For foreign and subsidiary rights, contact the author.

Cover design by: Martijn van Tilborgh

ISBN: 9781950718382   1 2 3 4 5 6 7 8 9 10

Printed in the United States of America

THE
PANIC
ROOM

PANIC, ANXIETY, AND THE
ART OF LYING TO EVERYONE

TROY MAXWELL

TABLE OF CONTENTS

INTRODUCTION

I sat by our bed while the walls seemed to close in around me. My heart pounded as if keeping up with some insane, unstoppable rhythm. Both my hands tingled, and my breaths came in gasps.

What is happening to me? I thought with a sharp sense of urgency. *I think I'm dying. This has to be the end.*

It was Sunday morning—the most important hours of my week. Normally I was up early getting ready, studying my message and heading over to the church. As the pastor, I was the only one who could do my part—bringing the teaching, leading the service, and loving the people with a handshake or a conversation after our two morning services. Yet here I was, my body and mind flashing emergency signals all over the place. I felt so debilitated that I didn't know if I had the courage to even leave my bedroom.

What if I get there and something happens in front of the congregation? I thought. *What if I have a heart attack while on the platform? I don't want people to have to witness that. How do I stop this thing?*

The sensation was like being in a room with no door handle, no way out. It was suffocating, pressing in on every side. My wife, Penny, was getting ready for the day as well, but there was no way I wanted to reveal to her what I was going through. She was my life partner in everything from marriage to ministry. Without her support and toughness, we never would have made it this far, but her opinion of me meant more than anyone else's. The last thing I wanted was to rattle her confidence in me. Now more than ever, I needed her to see me as a strong and reliable leader.

I stepped into our bathroom and steadied myself against the wall. My body and mind were reacting with high-level fear and anxiety, as if I were about to be hit by a train.

God, what is this? Please tell me, I prayed. *This can't happen, not now. You've got to pull me out of it. I'm spinning out of control.*

"Are you okay, Troy?" came Penny's voice through the door.

"Yeah, I'm fine," I said, trying to sound as confident as I could. My voice came out pretty normal, but maybe I had said the words too quickly.

"Okay," she replied with just a little hesitation. I hoped that I sounded well enough to put any suspicions to rest.

As she walked downstairs, I tried to reconnect with my routine of picking out clothes and shoes for the morning, mentally running through my message, and praying. But like waves breaking on a beach, panic rolled in and took over my thoughts. I sat down, clutched my head in my hands, and listened to my heart pound like a factory piston.

What is this thing? I asked God, and myself. *Is this the end of my ministry—or my life? Where will this all end?*

CHAPTER 1
THE COLLISION

I should have noticed the massive pressure building up in my life. In hindsight, it was all too obvious, maybe even predictable. But at the time it seemed normal, just like what everyone else goes through. I had signed up to be a leader and knew that being a leader could be very intense. Vacations are few, responsibilities are many, and my schedule was packed tight with stuff that seemed important. All of that and more blinded me to the fact that I was about to walk into a disaster.

Penny and I were in our fourth year as pastors of Freedom House Church which we had planted in Charlotte. Already the services were drawing several hundred people each weekend, and great things seemed to be happening. On this particular weekend, we had held our Strong Conference for men, an annual event with competitive games, teams, events, speakers, food, and all sorts of cool guy stuff. The theme that year was "Return" as we put the focus on returning to the things that got us where we were in the first place. Jesus told the church in Ephesus, "Return to your first love." We wanted that principle to really sink into guys' minds.

Three hundred to 400 men had converged on our campus for the weekend conference, and it went amazingly well. The sessions were super helpful, and the team games in the afternoon in the parking lot brought out the competitor in everyone. We ended the day with a big tug-of-war which was loud and raucous and fun.

The name of the conference, "Strong," and the theme, "Return," held a certain irony in light of what would slam into me just a few days later. My life was about to collide with a reality that challenged everything about my self-perception, my marriage, and my abilities as a leader.

The next day in church we celebrated with water baptisms, one of the best days in the life of any congregation. There's nothing like seeing people share a bit of their story, publicly declare their allegiance to Jesus, get dunked in the water as a picture of death and then rise from the water as a symbol of new life. Baptisms are amazing. They get me every time.

The celebratory atmosphere seemed to fit where we were as a congregation. Our church was looking toward a major move and was on the verge of buying 27 acres of land. This had been a major goal of ours since the founding of Freedom House. For a number of reasons, we couldn't keep meeting in a school building. Set-up and tear-down got old quickly and was wearing everybody out. More than that, people need a higher vision to stay engaged with the work of God. Nowhere in the Bible does it say the kingdom stays stagnant. Rather, the kingdom is always advancing, taking ground, doing greater things. People want to belong to a place that's going some-where, so their own lives become stronger and more effective along with the church they belong to.

Penny and I also knew that ambitious corporate goals train people's hearts. Some people only learn God-sized generosity when there is a God-sized need. Some only learn to have big vision for their lives when their church has a big vision for its future. The process of buying land, raising money, and building facilities was a great discipleship tool for training up godly leaders and families. There were so many lessons embedded in it.

In our context, this was especially important because most people who came to Freedom House were newly saved. We did not come to town intending to pull in transfer growth. We wanted to reach the un-churched and the over-churched, meaning those from other ministries who had been burnt out or hurt somehow. This created an interesting mix of people in our meetings who needed different types of leadership and care. One type needed to learn new things; the other needed to unlearn some old things. One needed an introduction to the faith, the other a kind of rehabilitation and return to the purity of first love. To inspire both types to grab onto the vision and support the church's future made for an interesting and healthy challenge.

Still, I love leading in challenging circumstances, and I'm more hands-on than most leaders. I like to be in the mix with people. If we had drawn seasoned Christians who simply wanted a new church to enjoy, I would have felt bored. But as it was, everything we did corporately was new to most of us, and people were on a faith journey with Penny and me. In that sense, the burden of leadership felt a little heavier. You don't want to let people down who are just learning to believe, or believe again.

The 27-acre property we were aiming for had been catching our eye for years. When our family had first moved to Charlotte, we would drive by this specific parcel between our home and the church. It had no "For Sale" sign and was zoned for industrial use. It was too big for a church of our size, and while I liked the vision it would inspire, I wasn't sure we could make it work financially.

Every time we would ride by, the property stood out to us. There was something about it we just couldn't explain.

Then, after a year or two, a "For Sale" sign appeared.

God, what do you want us to do? I prayed when I saw it. *Is this supposed to be our property?*

In the meantime, we didn't know if we should buy an existing facility, or maybe rent a better one, so we hired an agent but could find nothing that worked. Every time we made a step toward a certain property or rental, it fell through or Penny and I knew in our hearts that it wasn't the right direction.

Almost every day that we drove by the property between our house and the church, we found ourselves saying, "That's ours. We know we are supposed to buy that property." We would stretch our hands, extending our faith toward it and pray, believing that God would give it to us, somehow.

The idea of buying the huge parcel scared me. I had done all the research on the mortgage and how much we would have to raise. My professional background was in financial investments, so I had a heightened sense of what the numbers meant. It seemed way beyond our church's ability, maybe something for ten years down the line after we were better established. One thing that drove me crazy was driving around the city (any city, really) and seeing signs proclaiming, "Future home of Such-and-Such Church." Those signs often looked weathered and sun-beaten after about 15 years, and it was clear to everyone that the church had bought property but couldn't raise enough money to build on it. I consider that anti-vision. I can't imagine attending a church which has enough vision to buy land but not enough to see it all the way through. It would drain my energy and the people's faith week after week. I was determined not to get us into that kind of situation.

The growth God had sent us in a few short years seemed to confirm that He was doing something new and exciting in our city, and that raised my faith level. We approached the owners of the property and danced around with them about possible deals. We offered to buy part of the land, so they could retain some for industrial use, but we were not in a strong enough position to really dazzle anybody with what we brought to the table. Other buyers were interested in the whole property, so our discussions went nowhere.

Interestingly, all the other sales contracts kept falling through. Finally, after about three years, the owner called me.

"Troy, do you still want to buy this property?" he asked, seeming tired of the whole process.

"Absolutely," I said, "but you know the position the church is in financially. We can't match what others are bringing to the table, and banks aren't excited about lending us what we would need."

"What if I finance it for you?" he said. "If you come up with $200,000, I will finance the rest, $1.3 million, interest only for three years at three percent."

Wow, I thought. *That's an incredible deal.*

"That sounds pretty good," I said calmly, not wanting to portray too much excitement.

"I have to sell it," he said frankly. "If I don't do this, I will lose the tax deduction on it. I need that tax deduction."

"Let me get back to you," I told him.

I went to the board and the key givers in the church. The church had just $120,000 in cash, meaning we needed another $80,000 to make the deal. When I say we had $120,000, I mean that was all we had in the bank, not some separate building-fund account. To buy the property would eat up all our operating costs and put us essentially at zero. That was a pretty significant risk for a relatively new and unseasoned congregation.

Penny and I were in a similar position in our personal finances. We weren't making a lot of money as a family. In fact, we were living off our savings at this point. With the church almost doubling in size every year, we were emotionally and physically in the red. We weren't making a lot of money as a family. Our kids were young: now aged 4, 6, and 8. We weren't falling behind on our bills, but we certainly were not in a position to make major financial investments. It didn't feel like we had much margin anywhere.

But the church leaders were as fired up as we were by the possibility of owning the property and moving ahead to accommodate our rapid growth. So, we took a deep breath, entered into an agreement to buy the land and went through the steps to have it rezoned for church use. Soon we would have a large piece of land that needed a building on it. I wasn't about to put up a "Future Home of" sign. The clock was ticking. The closing date was less than a month away, and we did not have all the money we needed yet.

NIGHTMARE IN ANTIGUA

Planning meetings and financial conversations were at the forefront of my mind as the weekend of the conference came to a close and I packed my suitcase for Guatemala. I was heading there to help re-launch a church in Guatemala City with a series of meetings on a variety of topics. I didn't know the people at the church personally but had been recommended to them by a close ministry friend. The people wanted help growing their church and thought I could assist them because of what was happening with us in Charlotte. They also liked that I was an associate trainer with John Maxwell.

My flight was uneventful, and my host, a local business-man, showed me the church which was located in a nice part of Guatemala City and was drawing around 200 on a Sunday morning. All week long I spoke in daily meetings which were building up to what they hoped would be a big re-launch service at a hotel on Sunday. It was the kind of environment where everyone expected my advice on-demand and treated me like a visiting expert, even between sessions. I was also speaking on everything from leadership development to mar-riage ministry and felt pressure to be "on" all the time. When I was done speaking, the hosts would bring leaders up to ask me questions. I rarely had time to be alone, and it was more than a little overwhelming, with thoughts about the property back home occupying a good portion of my thoughts.

On Saturday night, they put me up in a hotel in Antigua, a gorgeous mountaintop city with cobblestone streets and an ancient air. The rooms were cabanas, the temperature much cooler than in the city, the pace more relaxed, and the views stunning. I had a little time to walk around and see Antigua, and then we had dinner at another amazing restaurant. The whole time I was thinking about my message the next day, one I had preached before, though not in Guatemala.

Back in my room, I emailed Penny and the kids, whom I really missed, watched a little TV, lay in bed and read over my preaching notes. To complicate things, I was preaching through a translator, which meant I had to condense everything to about half of what I wanted to say. I worked through my notes to highlight what I thought was most important.

All week long I had experienced trouble sleeping. A friend calls it "monkey mind." You lie down and try to sleep, and your mind races all over the map, thinking about this, that, and the other thing. Part of me was tremendously excited about the land we were about to buy but also stressed about raising the money. I'm not sure how much I slept that night, but I woke up to a vivid mountain morning on Sunday. The scenery was so beautiful it was hard not to stare at it. I ordered breakfast at the hotel restaurant—eggs, coffee, toast, juice—then waited for my ride to come take me to the big event.

And waited. And waited. Thirty minutes late, my host and another man pulled up in a small, sporty car.

"I'm sorry, my friend," he said. "I am late, but you will not be. We will get you there. Don't worry."

I don't like being late, so I climbed quickly into the back seat, and we began our descent on the serpentine road through the hills. Small talk began, and I went over my message in my head. Suddenly, I felt a strange sensation: motion sickness. I never had experienced motion sickness before, but as the host and his friend carried on pleasant conversation, and I tried to be cordial, I felt worse and worse.

"Pull over," I finally said, fearing I would vomit in the car. My host looked back, then veered to the side of the road, hit the brakes, and let me open my door. I hung my head out but didn't throw up. It felt terrible.

"What's wrong?" my host asked.

"Must be something I ate," I said. "Maybe the eggs."

"Switch seats," my host said. "Get in the front. Seeing the road will make you feel better."

I did, but as we resumed our trip it became clear that the motion sickness was not going away. Several times I asked him to pull over again. Small talk ceased as all three of us monitored my physical condition.

If I'm going to get food poisoning, people say it happens quickly, I thought, hoping the bad eggs—or whatever I had eaten—would resolve themselves and come out before the service started.

When we arrived at the hotel for the church meeting, music was playing and people were worshiping, but I hadn't improved one bit. I dragged myself into a back room they had for me, and someone brought Pepto-Bismol which I drank gratefully, hoping it would settle my stomach.

You have a job to do this morning, I told myself. *Just get right and do it.*

By faith, I stood up and gathered my notes to head into the meeting, but as I came to the threshold of the door leading into the main room, I found I couldn't go in. What felt like a physical barrier kept me from proceeding.

"I've got to..." I said by way of a weak explanation, and turned around. The people hosting me watched as I staggered into the bathroom.

I spent about ten minutes in the bathroom, trying to pull

myself together. I went back out and tried to walk through the main doors into the room where I would be speaking, but still I couldn't. By this time, my hosts were expressing open sympathy and concern. People brought me bottled water. Worship time continued, because I was the morning speaker, and I wasn't ready yet.

Troy, this can't go on, I told myself through the pain. *One more time, try to get that stuff out. Then it's "go" time.*

Another trip to the restroom yielded nothing, so with what felt like massive effort, I finally pushed through the barrier and into the meeting. Everything from that point on was a blur. They introduced me. I went up, thanked them, said something introductory, then spoke on the gospel account of the woman with the alabaster box. I said how awkward it could seem to be having dinner with someone when a prostitute comes in to wash your guest's feet with her hair, but for Jesus, this was a redemptive moment. Simon the Pharisee, his host, couldn't see it because he wasn't focused on Who was at the table—Jesus—but who was at Jesus' feet—this notorious woman. I even did an illustration using people from the congregation to simulate what that scene at the table might have looked like.

But I hardly remember any of it. I think it was well received, but I can't be sure. As soon as I was able to, I excused myself—possibly abruptly—made it to my room in that hotel (where I would be staying a few more days) and passed out for four hours.

When I woke up with shades drawn and silence filling the space, I tried to make sense of the experience. What had I felt? Incredibly sick for sure, but my stomach was okay now.

Maybe the Pepto had worked. Beyond that, there had been a strong desire to escape, to go away from there, and I didn't know how to make sense of that. The very walls had seemed to be closing in, and I actually feared that somehow I would die—from what, was unclear. Nothing in the environment was threatening. It was just me.

I had never experienced anything like it before. Glad that it was gone, I gave it no more thought as I relaxed for a few days. By the time I caught a plane home, that weird Sunday morning was in my rearview mirror.

THE SEQUEL IS ALWAYS WORSE

Back home, there was more work ahead. As soon as I landed, I got a new suitcase ready and packed into cars with fifteen other couples to drive south to Atlanta. Penny and I were leading a group from our church to a marriage conference which we were all attending together. Fortunately, I did not have to speak, but I would be "on" anyway as the leader of this group. The conference was on Friday and Saturday, and we would drive home Saturday night to be at our church on Sunday.

On the way to Atlanta, I explained in a little more detail to Penny what had happened to me in Guatemala City.

"Maybe it was the massage I got in Antigua," I said. "Maybe it was some sort of voodoo thing, and something demonic happened."

"Maybe it was a bad breakfast—or the water," she said. Neither of us could figure it out.

We enjoyed sessions all day Friday and Saturday, and Penny and I got to be with our main overseers and friends, Dennis and Colleen Rouse. As church leaders, we spent time in the green-room with people like Jimmy Evans and others we respected. By Saturday night, though, I recognized that I was completely out of energy. Exhaustion at some deeper level had come over me.

How am I going to handle services tomorrow? I wondered. *I'm so tired. I don't remember feeling like this before.*

Expecting to power through and take a nap later, I found myself on Sunday morning in a replay of the nightmare in Guatemala. My stomach felt like I had taken a swift kick to the gut. Sweat burst out all over my body. Walls, doors, and rooms felt like they were closing in around me. I noticed new symptoms, too: my heart raced, hands and feet tingled, and a certainty rose up in me that I was going to die.

I am having a heart attack, I told myself. *This is it. I'm going to die.*

I leaned over the toilet to try to vomit, but I couldn't. My body shook, my face was bright red, and Penny had the misfortune of walking in as I was gagging.

"What's happening?" she asked from the bathroom doorway. Even from my sideways vantage point I could read the concern on her face.

"I don't know," I said. "That same weird thing as in Guatemala. I don't know if I'm sick, or that lady put some evil spirit on me."

Penny stepped in and laid hands on me to cast anything

out that might be causing the affliction. My hands and feet kept tingling, my heart beat through my rib cage, and a sense of extreme nervousness took over my mind.

"What do you want to do?" she asked. "Do you want someone to step in and take the service?"

This wasn't a real suggestion. We both knew that our church was so young and so green that hardly anyone could step in if I went down.

"No, just get me to church," I said by faith. "Get me to church. I think this'll go away."

I repeated the hopeful prognosis, prayed prayers of self-deliverance, and tried to believe it all was doing some good.

Just get dressed and get there. I promised myself, *It'll stop at some point. It has to.*

I managed to get into the car with Penny and soon found myself standing in the front row at Freedom House during worship time. Usually that is an energizing, awesome moment. The few moments before I speak, I usually have a conversation with God. It's a time where I feel as if He reassures me of my calling and what I am about to do. It is an encouraging time. But all I could think of was how badly I wanted to run out of the building. I looked down at the black leather boots I had been looking forward to wearing. I was sure my pouring sweat was beginning to show through my clothing.

"Hey," I said, grabbing one of our pastors as he passed by. "Pray for me. Rebuke the sickness or voodoo or whatever it was that I picked up in Guatemala."

He laid hands on me and prayed, but nothing happened. In fact, I began to sweat so heavily that I knew I couldn't stay inside anymore. Trying to appear calm, I all but bolted out a side entrance, through a back door and into the cold morning air.

God, what is going on? I prayed helplessly. *What should I do?*

We were still meeting in an elementary school. Penny was serving in kids' ministry as she typically did on Sunday mornings. I stood there alone in the morning light, trying to catch my breath and hoping I wouldn't pass out and fall over.

My executive pastor, Makida, found me out there heaving. Her look told me, "This is pretty bad."

"I'm going to go get Pastor Penny," she said and disappeared through the door before I could offer any objection.

A minute later they both appeared. Penny put her gentle hand on my back and her face near mine.

"There's no way I can do this," I told her. "It's the same thing that happened before. I can't go back in there."

"Let's go into the back room," Penny suggested. I went with her and Makida and lay down, but my heart kept racing, fingers tingling, mind spinning with nothing to hold onto.

"I'm going into the service," I heard Penny say, and I knew what she was thinking: *The show must go on, and someone has to lead it.*

Worship time had already been extended because I wasn't ready to go, and in the auditorium, Penny signaled to the worship leader with a roll of her finger to continue. She was hoping I could get my act together and come in to preach.

Is he getting better or worse back there? she wondered. Images of me being rolled into an ambulance passed through her mind.

Soon it became clear that I wasn't going to appear.

I can't keep doing this rolling thing, Penny thought. *Where's Troy? Is he passed out? God, what's going on?*

Dutifully, she stepped up to the front and did everything she could to draw attention away from my situation.

"I'd like those couples who went on the retreat with us to come up and share about what happened in their lives," Penny said.

Those people did, and as they took turns speaking about what had happened, Penny prayed up a storm.

Holy Spirit, Troy needs to come, and he needs to come now, she said. But I didn't appear. It seemed obvious that people were wondering right along with her, *Where's Troy?*

Finally, after the testimonies, the service ended. Penny had emceed it all. In the back room, I felt well enough to come out to where everyone was and greet people, but a heavy sense of confusion, failure and shame came with me.

Here I am, the spiritual leader of the church and I can't do what I'm supposed to, I thought as I shook hands and smiled at people. Penny came up beside me.

"Are you okay?" she whispered.

"I'm fine," I said, summoning my remaining confidence. "I think it was just a dizzy spell or some weird spiritual thing. I think I'm good."

"That was really awkward," Penny answered. "I didn't know if you were going to have a heart attack and die."

Lord, what just happened to me? was the question ringing in my heart all the way home and for the rest of the day. *What is this thing? And how do I make it go away?*

The answer to that question was not the one I was expecting.

CHAPTER 2
SURVIVING CHILDHOOD

My upbringing had been anything but normal, and I often felt like an unlikely person to be leading a church, let alone one as blessed by God as Freedom House. I imagine I was like a lot of people who may have started their own business or tried to start something from scratch. I felt unqualified and inadequate.

My parents divorced when I was 14 months old. Mom was young and didn't have a car until she was 30, so we hitchhiked everywhere we wanted to go. She worked as a waitress for most of my upbringing, and much of the money she made went to drugs, which were everywhere in the apartment complex where we lived. Her money also went into the pockets of the unscrupulous boyfriends she always brought home.

Mom did all kinds of drugs, so I thought everybody in the world did. She worked late, and the guys she brought home would often sleep the day away in our apartment. Some were violent with her. When I was 12 or 13, Mom started dating a guy who was 18. By this time, Mom was letting me drink, and soon enough I was trying drugs as well—with her. At school, I was considered the cool kid because my mom bought alcohol and drugs for me, and we used together. Looking back, my childhood was crazy.

Dad was a trumpet player in a band called Ron Moody and the Centaurs. They had a #1 hit which put them on the map for a little while. I didn't know much about Dad's music career because he popped in and out of my life with little consistency. I knew he was a cool, good-looking guy who always had fun stuff going on, and he drove a Porsche for a long time.

His pattern for relating to me was to interject himself into my life suddenly, at unexpected times, and then leave a trail of broken promises.

"I'm going to start spending more time with you," he told me once, and I believed him. Then he was gone again for months.

Another time he showed up and gave me a gift of $100. The next day he came again and asked for the money back and went to the bar.

One time when I was eight, he promised he would come see me, and I sat on the back porch all day waiting for him to show up. He never did. That was how things were with my dad.

The one memorable season I had with him was when I was 12, and he brought me into his life at a horse farm. At 5 a.m. on Saturdays, he would pick me up to go riding. I remember standing in the kitchen in the farmhouse and having my first cup of coffee. It was instant coffee, and I watched Dad put cream and sugar in it, then hand it to me. It tasted so good.

Man, this is amazing! I thought. *I'm going to drink coffee the rest of my life, just like him.*

We spent those days riding horses together. I learned to ride English, to take care of horses, to work with saddles and bridles, and to jump. The farm owner raced horses in steeplechase-like events, and we watched them with a group of Dad's friends. We also hunted foxes on horseback.

Dad took me there on Fridays after work for a while, and partying seemed the glue that held everybody together. There was a regular group of men and women who came out every weekend to carouse more or less non-stop. When Dad was not drunk, he was kind, happy, endearing, and loving—the kind of man I wanted to be. But when he was drunk, which was often, his life became sad—and sometimes dangerous. After a weekend of drinking all the way through until Sunday, Dad would be too sauced to drive me home but tried anyway. Many times he went off the road, and I was sure we would die.

"Dad, do you want me to drive?" I asked, at just 13 years old. But he somehow managed to get me back to Mom's apartment every time. I liked being with Dad, but the bad times always outweighed the good.

When I was 15 or so, Dad decided he wanted another shot at being a full-time father and asked my mom if I could come live with him. Mom was excited. She was ready to not have me in the house or in her life, so I moved into Dad's apartment across from my high school. Dad had just finished a mysterious business venture that had gone south. He had borrowed $80,000 to start a sandwich shop in Lynchburg, Virginia, at a cool spot in a mall. But the business had failed. Now he was back in Richmond and had landed a great job as a computer coder for the FDIC, the federal banking system. He was making $60,000 or more a year in the 1980s, which was a lot of money then.

The problem was, he still drank heavily every night. There were many nights I would come home to a passed-out father. He had drunk two—sometimes three—bottles of wine. Again, I thought it was great at the time because I got to drink too. I partied regularly with him and with my friends, and nobody told me it was bad.

Then Dad's drinking and horseback riding combined in a nearly fatal way. I got a call one day at home where I was hanging out with a friend. It was Dad's parents.

"Your dad has been in a horse accident," they said. "He's in the hospital, and it doesn't look good."

Someone took me to the hospital, and I could see they were right. Dad had suffered a third-degree head trauma. He had been riding drunk, without a helmet, fallen off the horse onto a fence and landed on his head.

Wow, this is bad! I thought.

Over time he had to relearn basic functions and was in rehabilitation for a year or two. He lost his job and became totally disabled.

Everything went downhill from there. His alcoholism grew worse. I couldn't live with him anymore, and Mom didn't want me back because it had been a couple of years, and she had her life and a new boyfriend. In the back of my mind, I wanted some semblance of a normal family, so I elected to move in with my dad's parents since they had offered.

WALKING IN HIS FOOTSTEPS

Dad's parents were very much involved in my life from that point on. They felt guilty over how my dad had turned out, and I provided them with something of a second chance. I found out later that they paid his child support until I was an adult. They also took me to church, but it was more dead religion than a living faith for them.

Meanwhile, Dad went from town to town along the East Coast living off his disability check and stealing money from people by lying to them. He told them he was part of the Maxwell House coffee family and gave them an "opportunity" to invest. He could be very persuasive and charming. I would often get phone calls from women who said, "I'm looking for Tom Maxwell, and he left me your number. He owes me $5,000. He told me he would invest it in the Maxwell coffee fortune."

I would respond, "You lost your money. You're never going to get it back. He lied to you." That happened often. Businesses would call about checks he had bounced. Worse, he would cycle back around and become abusive toward his own parents, trying to bully them into giving him money. Many times he and I almost got into fistfights when he would show up drunk and try to somehow get their money.

I finished high school living with them, and my grandfather told me he would pay for my college. I applied to a bunch, but I was drinking all the time and on top of that was a very bad test-taker. No college would accept me, so I went to summer school at VCU (Virginia Commonwealth University). The college allowed me to take a few classes in the summer which would allow me to enroll in the fall.

Money started coming in when I turned eighteen because Dad was disabled, and I was a beneficiary. I also had a good job working as a bank teller. At the bank, I met Bubba and Doug, guys a little older than I was, and we moved in together in the Fan, a neighborhood just outside of Richmond. It was a hip area, and I was living the highlife while I worked and went to college. Bubba gave me his driver's license, and I made a fake ID, so I was now "21," and started living even crazier, like they did.

I joined a fraternity after my lease was up with Bubba and Doug, and five of us fraternity brothers moved into a huge house in downtown Richmond. My goal was to be a millionaire by age 30, but my lifestyle was taking me down fast. Soon, I ran out of money altogether—partying obliterates your bank account at some point—and ended up moving back in with my grandparents.

One night I drove home really drunk and really high. I don't know how I made it. It was 2 or 3 a.m. when I walked up the stairs of their house to my bedroom—the one my dad had grown up in. As I turned the corner and saw myself in a mirror, I realized my dad was looking back at me. I was becoming the very person he was. Drunk all the time. Irresponsible. Needing money. Soon—who knows?—I might even become abusive to those around me. That was a future too bitter for me to contemplate.

I didn't know a thing about God, but that became my "Prodigal Son" moment. Somehow, someway, I would do everything I could to avoid the path my father was on. The only problem was I didn't have any idea how.

CHAPTER 3
DIAGNOSING
THE VOODOO

Maybe I'm still tired or sick from Guatemala, I thought on that first, disastrous Sunday when I had failed to preach and left Penny holding the bag.

I had gone home afterward, slept for a while, and everything seemed better. If it were some lingering illness or weird spiritual thing, I was sure it would fade away as I rested, prayed, and eased into a normal pace.

"Troy, you're exhausted," some close associates on staff told me the next day. "You need a break."

At their suggestion, I took our family for a stay-cation at the Embassy Suites on the other side of Charlotte. It was fun being with Penny and the kids, but I was still doing work stuff, and anytime a leadership responsibility came up, I felt debilitated and unable to engage. The next Sunday morning, I woke up to the sequel of what had happened before: heart racing, walls closing in, fear of death gripping my heart, limbs tingling. This time I wasn't willing to make Penny carry the morning or let people go home disappointed because they hadn't heard the Word of God preached, so I summoned all my wits and pressed through. I taught on finances, and between services I hid in the back room and had a pretty blunt conversation with God.

What is going on with me? I demanded. *Why is this happening? What is it?*

This time God actually responded, and His response struck me as bizarre.

I want you to call Jay Zinn, He spoke to my heart.

Jay Zinn was a friend of mine, somewhat older than I, who pastored River's Edge Church in Davidson, a suburb of Charlotte. I knew Jay well. When our family moved to Charlotte, he and I went to lunch and spent time getting to know each other. He had grown a church in another city, handed it over to someone else, and started his church at around the same time we started Freedom House.

What in the world does Jay have to do with anything? I asked God and was met with silence.

As I joined Penny on the front row during second-service worship, I leaned over to her.

"I feel like God told me to call Jay Zinn," I said.

"Why?" she asked.

"I don't know," I said.

Fear still gripped me, and when it was time I willed myself into the pulpit to get through my second message. Right when I got home, I called Jay.

"Jay, I don't know what's going on with me," I said.

"What's happening?" he asked.

I explained what had happened in Guatemala and since I got home. When I finished, he said calmly, "Troy, you're having a panic attack."

"What?" I exclaimed. I didn't even know what he meant. I had heard mention of panic attacks and anxiety attacks, but I thought they were for people with severe psychological problems.

"You're having a panic attack," he repeated.

"I thought I was just sick or tired or something," I replied.

"No. I've had them. Everything you're describing happened to me," he said. "It's your frontal lobe releasing adrenaline, causing a fight or flight response. Your brain thinks there is danger, and it's trying to deal with it."

"But I'm not nervous about anything," I protested.

"Troy, it's way different than that," he said almost reassuringly. "There's much more to it."

I still wasn't sure I believed him, but I knew God had told me to call him.

"Then, what do I do?" I asked.

"Make a doctor's appointment tomorrow morning," Jay said with almost relaxed authority. "See the doctor, and he'll get you on a medication that will help you navigate this until you understand what's going on in your mind and body. Then, you can look at how to treat it long-term."

Reluctantly, but also a little hopefully, I heeded his words and found myself in a doctor's office. I described my symptoms, and the doctor listened nodding.

"Panic attacks," he said when I was finished. "You are describing panic attacks. People have them because adrenaline is released when a threat is perceived. When someone lives with stress for a long period of time, it wears out their adrenal glands which produce serotonin and melatonin, the feel-good and sleep hormones. Adrenal failure finally occurs when the glands stop functioning well. Basically, when you wear yourself out emotionally and physically, your body responds to emergencies that don't exist."

"Well, what's the answer?" I asked him.

"The long-term answer is a healthier lifestyle," he said. "To help you get there, I recommend starting on medication to settle your brain down, so panic attacks are less likely."

I didn't like the sound of that at all. The idea of going on medication for a problem I had caused—and which I should be able to control—seemed tantamount to failure. But the idea of having another panic attack was even more terrifying.

"Is there any other way, aside from medication?" I asked.

The doctor shrugged and shook his head, "Not really. You could ride it out and see if it goes away on its own."

I imagined what that looked like. I could not live in fear of another panic attack without giving myself a fighting chance.

"Okay," I said after hesitating. "I'll try it."

He prescribed a long-term anti-depressant, Lexipro, and a short-acting one, Xanax, if a panic attack happened. I had never taken medication regularly before and had no idea what to expect. Within weeks, it seemed to help keep negative emotions in check. The dread of having a panic attack receded. In a way, I got my life back.

But the price was a sort of numb feeling. No real highs. No real lows. Emotional distance and disinterest. Little interest in relationships. Fewer feelings. A muted sex life.

In all honesty, I hated it.

All the while, my mind was trying to make sense of what had actually occurred to cause the panic attacks—if that was what they were. I am by nature a linear, logical person. I want to understand things, to break them down. So what was going on with me? Had I suffered a mental breakdown? If so, why was it isolated to certain situations and contexts?

My mind ran through many possibilities. Did I have sin I needed to confess? Was this divine punishment? If not, why would God let me experience this? Wasn't I giving my life to serve Him and His people? What was the root cause? Was it a spiritual attack? Was it fatigue?

I knew I wasn't going through any kind of depression, at least I didn't think so. Exciting things were happening in our lives, and I was enjoying the opportunities ahead of me. I didn't think long-term stress was the cause. I was a leader. This stuff came with the territory. It was the responsibility God had given me. I should be able to manage it.

My logic spun round and round, but I kept those internal conversations to myself. Meanwhile, I realized that the medication did not totally remove the fear of having another panic attack. Every leadership moment, meeting, decision-making situation, or speaking demand threw my mind into overdrive.

Is it coming? Is that the start of a panic attack? When's it going to hit? Now? Maybe when I get up to speak?

It was like being stalked and never knowing when the predator was going to strike. Fear created its own weather pattern in my soul, stirring up anxiety and becoming a self-fulfilling prophecy. Thoughts swirled in my head, all pointing to my failure.

I let God down.

I let Penny down.

I let my church down.

I let myself down.

I'm damaged goods.

I won't ever be normal again.

This is the end of my ministry and all our dreams.

I'm not strong enough to beat this.

High on my list of frustrations was what the panic attacks and the medications were doing to my relationship with Penny, whose respect I craved more than any other person's.

MEETING IN THE JUNGLE

I had met Penny in the fall of my senior year in college when this knock-out blonde girl walked into the fraternity party we were having. I saw her from across the room and said to myself, *I'm gonna marry that girl.* It was a jungle-themed party, the biggest one on campus, which explains why I was dressed like a tree with vines all over me, and wearing nothing else but a Speedo. Penny was only there to drive some of her friends around. She was not a drinker. When she saw the drunk guy dressed like a tree coming over to hit on her, she wanted nothing to do with him.

In the limited conversation I was able to draw out from her, I learned she was attending Oral Roberts University and had come back to Richmond for a while after breaking up with her boyfriend. Soon, she left the party with her friends, but I couldn't stop thinking about her.

I started seeing her everywhere on campus and made no secret that I was interested in dating her. I think she finally agreed because I wore her down. We started going out, and by the fifth date I thought I was getting somewhere. My motivations were not entirely holy. Penny took me to the park for a little heart-to-heart.

"Listen," she began, "I'm not really interested in you. I'm looking for a guy who is on fire for God."

Her words made no sense to me.

"First of all," I responded, "I don't even know what that means. Second of all, you haven't even given me a chance to be 'on fire for God.'"

She continued, "I want someone who wants to go to church with me."

Seems simple enough, I thought.

"Fine, I'll go," I replied.

"You will?" she said, surprised.

"Yeah, I want to try it out," I said, which was not completely untrue.

Having virtually no spiritual background, I thought all churches were the same. A few hours a week was a small price to pay to date a girl I was head over heels for. But Penny's church was different in ways I couldn't even describe. There was something "other" there—life, a tangible presence, an atmosphere way beyond anything I had experienced. I started attending on Sundays and Wednesdays and met cool guys my age, which surprised me as well.

A few weeks into my church-going career, a guy named Dennis Rouse spoke his final sermon at Penny's church before heading off to Bible school. He had been Penny's youth pastor before that. That night rocked my world. Dennis concluded with an altar call, inviting people to get saved and receive the baptism of the Holy Spirit. I came forward and was immediately delivered of alcohol. I was radically reborn. Everything in my life changed in a moment.

Back at the fraternity house—where I was on the council and well known as one of the crazier partiers—I didn't know what to do with myself. I was in two different worlds and had to remove myself from the fraternity world because I didn't want to live that way anymore. Thankfully, I was living with my grandparents and not in the fraternity house itself. Still, things felt disorienting and schizophrenic. I tried to talk to my old friends about Jesus and the change He had made in me, but they weren't interested. They were in full-on party mode, and they were mad at Penny for messing me up. In the end, I had to walk away from those relationships and leave that environment behind.

Church became my home away from home. It had all kinds of fun opportunities and events, and Penny and I were there constantly. I found a whole new set of friends to hang out with while doing ministry stuff. It was a church with about 1,200 people and growing exponentially. The congregation soon built a $28 million building with 4,500 seats, and big names spoke there. Penny and I did everything we could—worked with children, youth, and young adults, led marriage groups, started ministries from scratch—and were very involved in reaching the poor.

But the biggest transformation in my life came from reading the Bible and falling in love with the Word of God. I have never gotten over my love for the Bible, and I was surrounded by people who were on the same journey.

Penny and I were married two years after we met, and I learned that our backgrounds were very different. I came from a poor dysfunctional family. She came from a wealthy dysfunctional family. She had been abused physically, emotionally, and sexually by her grandfather, and the family never chose to confront him about it, though he preyed on others as well. My childhood was different, but no less troubled.

We were looking forward to creating together a healthier

life than either of us had enjoyed up to that point. Very much in love, and believing strongly in each other, we moved into a small apartment after our wedding. I worked in sales and found my stride as a certified financial planner, helping people with their investments and insurance. Penny worked at a bank and in a restaurant. Life was fun, especially when I won some trips for being the "Rookie of the Year" at work. Then I moved to another company and did well there, too. Eventually, I went out on my own in the investment business.

Our first child, Colby, arrived in 1997. This was a big step of faith because Penny had been diagnosed with polycystic ovarian syndrome—cysts on the ovaries that make it difficult to have children. When God blessed us with Colby and we stepped into parenthood, faith became a lifestyle for us.

Penny became pregnant again in 1998, and this time we had significant issues because our daughter, Cabell, was diagnosed in utero with tumors in her brain. The ultrasound doctor sat us down with a box of tissues and showed us pictures of Cabell's brain.

"You're going to have a little girl," she said. "Now look at this picture. Her brain is all gray. It's supposed to be black. It's gray because your daughter has tumors all through her brain."

Penny and I sat there stunned but not willing to agree with the negative diagnosis.

"One of two things can happen," the doctor continued. "Your baby can be born with Down's Syndrome, or with Edwards' Syndrome (Trisome 18), a chromosomal condition that could possibly affect many parts of her body. The only way we can test to find out which one she will have is by doing an amniotic fluid test. But she will have one or the other."

I'll never forget Penny's quiet reply in that moment.

"I don't want to do that. I believe our child will be healed."

I was so proud of her and in total agreement. She and I clasped hands and prayed right there in the room with the doctor. Somehow we both knew that God would heal Cabell. In any case, we couldn't do anything but believe.

It was not an easy couple of months as we trusted God with our unborn baby's healing. We went back to the hospital nearer the time of her birth for another ultrasound. The same ultrasound doctor came in and sat down, again with a box of tissues.

"I don't know how to explain this," she said. "This time the box of tissues is for me. This is a miracle. This baby is completely healed. I have never seen anything like this in my life."

She showed us pictures of Cabell's brain, and it was completely clean. Our baby girl was born healthy, happy, and without problems. We had experienced an undeniable miracle which caused our faith to soar even higher as we went into the future as a family.

MOVE INTO MINISTRY

In those years, my passion for volunteering at church had grown to something more: a desire to transition into some type of full-time ministry. Penny and I, as unpaid volunteers, had spent six years helping in youth ministry and had grown the group from 30 to about 300 people. I was making a lot of friends with guys who traveled and ministered and came to preach at our church. I liked the idea of doing what they did, traveling and preaching, while keeping my job to help support us. I had already gone all over the world taking teens on mission trips and had developed something of a preaching gift.

I raised money to do some overseas crusades but was having a hard time getting that ministry off the ground. Nothing was developing as fast as I wanted it to. So I traveled with other ministers to serve as an assistant and to observe them. I saw great miracles of blindness and deafness healed, plus much more.

God, when will you release me to be an evangelist like these men? I prayed over and over again. No answer came. Then one day in the midst of my frustration over my future in ministry, God dropped a dream in my heart.

I want you to plant a church, He spoke to me.

Immediately, I envisioned a church where the power of God was present, but one which felt culturally more connected to un-churched people. I pictured a place with great teaching and music, a place you would want to invite your friends, and a place where signs, wonders, and the gifts of the Spirit took place in the context of everyday life. The place I was picturing didn't seem to exist yet—and I felt an invitation to build it. I told Penny, and she too got excited for the vision.

As happens when God transitions you from one assignment to another, I suddenly saw things at our church that I thought I could do better. As much as I loved our church, I did not feel comfortable inviting an unsaved person into that environment. Why? Because it was so different from the way things worked, looked, and sounded outside the four walls of the sanctuary. I knew it wasn't the ministry of the Holy Spirit that was the problem, but the way it was stewarded by the leaders. There was little effort to create an environment where things were taught or explained to newcomers. Rather, things of the Spirit just happened and could often have seemed totally alien to those who might be visiting.

Penny and I wrestled with questions about what the ministry of the Holy Spirit looks like. We read the Bible with fresh eyes to gain new insight. Meanwhile, we began to share with close friends and colleagues our dream of planting a church, and to our surprise, nobody was buying it. Most guys we told about it actively discouraged us. One specifically, who was a great communicator and minister, shook his head when I told him what was on our hearts.

"Man, don't do it," he said. "You've got a great thing going here. You need to stay right where you are."

"But I feel like God's telling me to step out and pioneer this way," I protested.

"No, it's not God," he assured me.

I had learned by then that there are certain things you learn from people and certain things you don't. No one individual will give you all the right advice and counsel. You have to sift through people's words to hear God's voice.

I thank God for resources like Rick Warren's *Purpose-Driven Church* that helped us dream big. It showed me that when creating a place that unsaved people want to try, the way you talk and operate personally and as a church body has to be thought out and attractive. I discovered a couple of churches that were moving in that direction, so we learned all we could and took our journey one step at a time.

The biggest faith-building experience for Penny and me was still the miracle that had saved Cabell. More than anything, that gave us the ability to believe that God would again do the impossible.

"God," we prayed, "if you could heal our daughter from massive brain problems, we know you can help us plant a church with no money and no friends in a place where we have no connections or roots."

God directed us to start the church in Charlotte, North Carolina, a place neither of us had spent any real time in, and where we knew virtually no one. God's ways are not our ways, but we prepared to obey Him by making one of the biggest moves of our lives.

It was the beginning of a journey that would turn out surprisingly well—from a growth perspective—and difficult when it came to the effects I was feeling now.

CHAPTER 4
THE WALL

When I went to the doctor at Jay Zinn's recommendation, I weighed 220 pounds, and my eating habits were taking me down a road to soon being much heavier than that. Fast food was normal fare for me, and I was so ignorant about what healthy food was that I thought ordering a fried chicken sandwich at Wendy's instead of a hamburger was a positive lifestyle choice. Sodas and sweet tea were my constant companions, as was caffeinated coffee and a variety of junk foods too embarrassing to mention.

"If you want to get this under control, you have to do some things physically," the doctor told me. "Lose some weight, exercise and improve your diet."

"Will that get me off the medication sooner?" I asked him.

"It will help," he said.

I'm an all-in kind of person, so I made immediate changes. My goal was to deal with the anxiety head-on and overcome it rather than stubbornly hold on to old habits and live under the shadow of panic attacks for the rest of my life. But change wasn't easy. Salads don't give the same satisfaction as chicken sandwiches—at least not at first. And when you're used to drinking sugar water all day in the form of soft drinks and sweet tea, your body wonders what happened when suddenly it's gone.

Not to mention caffeine. I quickly discovered that it was a

huge crutch for me. Any stimulant worsens panic symptoms, and here I was guzzling it day after day. Coffee was the hardest thing to cut back on, a measure of how much my body and mind relied on it. Soon I was allowing myself to drink only water and limited amounts of coffee. I started a high-protein, low-carb diet and ate sweets moderately.

I also threw myself into exercise, starting with a home workout series called P90X. The first workout killed me. It involved doing a murderous number of push-ups and pull-ups—three pull-ups, to be exact. Even then, I couldn't raise my arms over my head without major pain the next day.

At first, the results were nothing. But after the sixth week, something shifted and my body started to get with the program. The fat started to go away and muscle emerged. Hungry for more progress, I did other video workouts as well, and I brought them to work so people on staff could join me at 6 a.m. for pre-workday workouts in a little space in our building. When it was warm, we did it outside. We had positive competitions for metrics like body-fat percentage, and we kept it fun and inspiring. It felt good to help others lock in to good habits as well.

After a while, I got tired of video workouts because I could repeat everything the workout leaders said, so I joined a local gym and used the principles I had learned to create my own workout regimens. I lifted weights, did cardio training, and put strategies like muscle confusion and metabolic conditioning into practice. Four or five days a week I was at the gym playing racquetball and tennis. I even swam a little bit because there was an aquatic center there.

Within a year, I lost more than twenty pounds and my waist went from 36 inches to 32 inches. When I went through security at the airport, they looked hard at my driver's license wondering, *Is that really you?* I tend to carry extra weight in my face, so the "new Troy" looked a lot different than the "fat Troy" pictures of the past.

I realized that planting Freedom House had taken the place of being active. My schedule had been way out of whack for years as I worked 60-80 hours a week. Long hours meant eating on the job and not really doing anything physically healthy. For the first time in a long time, I enjoyed being in my own body and looked forward to the little habits of caring for my temple.

That said, I wish it had been a straight line from diagnosing the panic attacks to overcoming them with positive lifestyle changes. It wasn't. The problems behind the attacks went a lot deeper than I knew. The truth is, though the changes in my life were good and real, I still did not feel normal. I wasn't having many panic attacks after going on medication, but the symptoms threatened me without fully rising to the level of an actual attack. It was very strange and kept me in a sort of emotional limbo, trying to manage each day, each decision, each interaction successfully. Imagine trying to not think of the thing you don't want to think about. That soaked up much of my energy. In that sense, it was still controlling my life.

As a result, I wasn't leading or pastoring the church well. And I wasn't being the husband I could be either. I was trying to excuse away the thought that I needed to be on medication. In some ways, I was in denial about how serious it all was, in essence, lying to myself and others.

THE JOURNEY TO THE SURFACE

As anyone knows who has had one, a panic attack makes you feel that there is no way out, that you're under water, trapped. I like to surf, and one thing I learned in the water is to avoid the whitewash zone where waves crash one after another and easily overwhelm you. I have been there before, pushed underwater over and over until it's hard to get a breath. You end up fighting to make it to the surface to get the oxygen you need to stay alive.

There are only two ways I know of to get out of the whitewash zone: ride a wave in and start all over, or dive underneath a wave and swim against the current. The latter is a lot of work, but either one is better than staying there, going under until you're too weak to fight.

Panic attacks made me feel like I was in the whitewash zone with no strategy to get free: one wave after another pushing me under, body panicking, mind cycling out of control, and external forces winning the battle to keep me submerged. Even the closed-in feeling of the water felt the same as what I felt in a panic attack as my mind perceived the world around me growing smaller, pressing in, robbing me of free movement.

The difference was that in the water I actually might have physically drowned. In a panic attack, my mind just believed it was so. My mind acted as if I were constantly in the whitewash zone, paddling to keep my head above water and spending all my energy to overcome fear of the waves. It was debilitating.

Of course, there were things I could do to fight it. I knew to concentrate and tell myself there was nothing wrong. I spoke the promises of God out loud, over and over. I assured myself

I had no reason to be afraid in this situation. I took big, deep breaths. I pictured God with me in the moment. But it took a lot of work and left little energy for everything else.

It was hard for me to believe, but the church kept growing, kept moving forward, kept thriving as if there were nothing wrong with me. A lot of that, I now realize, was due to Penny's leadership, but at the time it made me feel like I was completely better. If you had asked me how I was doing, I would have said, "I feel great." And I believed it. I had talked myself into an "I'm good" frame of mind which wasn't based in reality.

And the people closest to me, especially Penny, knew something wasn't right. I was "off." The panic attacks themselves, plus the side effects of the medication, plus my anxious desire to avoid panic attacks, overtook my personality. Few people on my staff knew. For two years I put up a good front, plowed through, and pretended all was well. It became an art.

THE SHAME OF SHARING

For me, one of the greatest barriers to getting better was simply telling Penny what was wrong. Maybe other guys are like me—admitting my weaknesses to my wife is harder than to a guy friend. I want her to see me as strong, confident and courageous. I want her to see me as a bold father and a good leader, pastor, husband and mate. To say, "I don't know what's going on with me, and I can't do what I need to do," was more than my self-esteem could take. It meant acknowledging that I was less than the man I could be, or that I wasn't capable of fulfilling God's call on my life. That was the worst feeling in the world.

This is probably why more guys don't pray with their wives. It requires an intimacy, an admission of need, an openness about weakness that most men don't like. I certainly did not want to look weak, incapable, and paralyzed in front of Penny. The best way to handle it was to lie to her and say, "I'm fine," when really I was not fine at all, and she knew it.

To make it more complex, our church background together was one in which you didn't admit sickness, financial need or any other negative thing. You had to couch it by saying things like, "I'm not feeling well in the natural, but by the stripes of Jesus I am healed." The idea was never to speak anything outside of faith, because your words determine your reality. And yet we had seen some messed-up things in some churches. One pastor's family, kids, and marriage were in terrible condition while the church was booming. He created a doctrine that said, "God gave me the ministry first, just like God gave Adam the garden before He gave him Eve." This was biblically inaccurate. God told "them" to have dominion. This man's excuse was a fig leaf over the fact that his family was falling apart, and he had wrong priorities. He built a doctrine around his dysfunction.

Another complicating factor was that Penny and I were in uncharted ministry territory, as pioneers always are. We were taking spiritual ground in a new city, trying to define a new expression of church and facing some serious spiritual resistance. Few congregations grew as quickly as ours, and people looked to us as an inspiring example of innovation. While Penny and I had some level of preparation and support from friends in ministry who had experienced a similar growth curve, nothing prepared us personally for the wear and tear it caused. The truth is, you don't even notice the wear and tear when things are going well. You tell yourself,

"I'm successful. God is blessing everything." *Momentum and success hide weaknesses which persist under the surface.* When you are experiencing success, you don't even think to look for what's wrong—and you don't want to. The first time you discover a weakness is when something breaks. That was a naïve perspective on our part.

A perfect illustration of this was the really nice, two-story, stainless steel Thermador oven in the house we bought. It was a great oven, but after a while it wasn't heating like it should. We called the warranty company and they said, "It's not fixable. We'll give you $5,500 to buy a new one." We got the money and decided to put it toward other things while continuing to use the oven, which was partially working. Penny is an accomplished cook and author of cookbooks, and I honor her for dealing with that thing. She had to move food around to get it to cook right, and she made it work, but the oven made a beeping noise every time it cooled down. You had to go up and hit it to make it stop. Over time, our family understood exactly when it would start beeping and where to hit it. One day, I became so tired of the beeping that I pulled off the panel and tried to make the beeping stop. In that process, I broke the oven the rest of the way, and we *had* to buy a new one.

My life was like that oven. Things were working a little bit, and though I still looked fine on the outside, the persistent beeping was a warning signal that not all was well. When the problem finally became unmanageable and I tried to address it, everything else seemed to break.

The only difference was that, with panic attacks, I wasn't yet ready to pull the cover off my life and fix what needed fixing. In fact, I did the opposite. After four or five years, I began to wean myself off the medication, which had always been a source of shame for me. Medication gave me the false impression that I was getting a handle on things. I figured diet and exercise changes were working. Medication only masked the beeping. I was still preoccupied, not fully present. Emotionally, Penny and I were out of sync. I was messed up and didn't know it.

It was like being in the fog of war. We were trying to figure out what our reality looked like as a married couple and as co-pastors of our fast-growing church—both within the context of the problem I was pretending didn't exist. For Penny, my reality was plenty ugly. I'll let her tell it.

CHAPTER 5

ON THE OTHER SIDE OF PANIC ATTACKS

He's on medication now. Things will go back to the way they were, I thought after Troy's diagnosis. *Disaster averted.*

The two nightmare Sundays were behind us. Troy and his doctor had implemented the right medication regimen, and the anxiety was under control. I breathed a sigh of relief.

But as time went by, I could tell the diagnosis was hitting Troy hard. When I tried to dig a little bit and see what he was feeling, his responses to me were clipped. The wall went up. I figured he was sorting through feelings, but I wanted him to know I admired him as much as I always did, and respected him as my husband and the leader of our home as well as our church. I wanted clear communication, vulnerability—some sense of what he was going through—so I could walk through it with him.

Vulnerability was not what Troy wanted at that time. He was clearly preoccupied with not having another panic attack. As time progressed, his schedule and priorities changed dramatically, leaving me in charge of things I wasn't planning on leading. When he unilaterally began to wean himself off medication, his symptoms returned, and I began to feel like a victim of his panic attacks even though I wasn't the one having them. He was in a room created by walls of fear and shame. I was outside the room trying to get through a door that was barred from the inside.

ENABLING THE DISABLEMENT

For the first three years after Troy's attacks began, I had a lot of compassion for him.

We've been plowing for six years without a vacation, and the church is growing so fast that it's no wonder we feel stress, I told myself. *Troy got injured somehow in the process of building this ministry. You can't expect someone with a broken leg to run a marathon. We have to let it heal.*

Grace felt easy because as much as Troy and I both have strong personalities, I have always tried to embrace my Proverbs 31 mandate: to make his name great in the gates. If he was struggling a little bit, I didn't tell anyone else because I didn't want to dishonor his name or our family or ministry. So only a few people on our staff knew, and we didn't initially tell the church board or even some of our closest friends.

But it seemed to me that Troy was increasingly cloudy, foggy, not processing decisions well. Even talking about panic attacks would send him into denial mode: "I'm fine, I'm fine." Yet sometimes it was all he could do to prepare a message and deliver it on Sundays at our two services. He wasn't enjoying ministry much, if at all. I understood that, and sometimes felt the same way, but it didn't make our ministry responsibilities disappear.

ON THE OTHER SIDE OF PANIC ATTACKS

I started watching for patterns of behavior and noticed he was unable—or unwilling—to process situations that had potential for conflict. He also had a hard time seeing something all the way through to the finish. Instead of going A to Z, he went A to F and handed it off to me or someone else. Sometimes, he simply made a bad decision.

Why is he not able to see that this is a really bad decision? I wondered. *Is this temporary? Is he just getting his confidence back? Where's the old Troy?*

As his symptoms persisted, my mind searched for answers:

Is this early-onset dementia?
Is it something hereditary?
Just stress?
A normal guy thing?
A middle-age thing?
Does he need a vacation?
Does he have too much on his plate?
Does it have to do with drugs he used as a teen?
Is there something biologically wrong with him?

Sometimes our kids looked to me for answers when Troy came across as clueless. I kept returning to the same position: "He's going through something, and I don't fully know what it is, but it's only a season, and until it passes, I won't ever put him in a bad light."

That being said, I did tell myself, *If he goes out and buys a little red sports car, that's it. I'm not standing by for any mid-life crisis.*

PROCESS VS. DENIAL

From the beginning of our relationship, Troy's and my communication styles have been very different. In Troy's family you denied and avoided everything, sweeping difficult stuff directly under the rug. In mine, the person who shouted the loudest won, so I learned to argue well and not back down. In addition to that, my mom and dad had eight marriages between them, so Troy and I had no concept of what a healthy marriage looked like. We had to learn everything from the ground up. Combining our two styles has taken a lot of grace and a lot of work.

We made a smart decision early on to get into counseling before we needed it. We were always pouring our hearts and lives into other people and didn't want to become blind to our own problems. We called it taking our vitamins in advance rather than getting treatment later. In one of our first counseling meetings, the counselor asked both of us, "Tell me about childhood traumas you had." I rattled off twenty-five things off the top of my head. Then we turned to Troy.

"I don't really have anything," he said in all seriousness. "I had a pretty normal childhood."

My jaw dropped.

"What are you talking about?" I blurted out. "You watched someone assault your mom. Your dad left you multiple times on a doorstep saying he'd come back and never did. He gave you one gift your whole life, then took it back so he could drink. Your mom sold drugs and used them—with you. You hitchhiked because you had no car, and you went to live with your grandparents who had no rules."

Troy listened and said, "Oh, I guess you're right."

He meant it.

When we had kids, our personality differences stood out even more. Our kids would ride bikes in the street, but I knew there was a pizza-delivery guy who flew through our cul-de-sac, and we had to watch out for him. Troy made me feel like I was overreacting.

"It's not a big deal," he would say.

Then one day when the kids were two and four, the pizza-delivery guy came flying through and Troy literally grabbed one of the kids off the tricycle to save him from harm. The trike rolled over into a ditch, and I looked at him like, "No big deal, huh?"

Like a lot of women, I wear my heart on my sleeve and process verbally. When things happen, I talk about them, and it helps. But when the counselor asked Troy how he had processed the negative experiences from his childhood, Troy shrugged and said, "I just push through and don't let stuff bother me." That was so true. Whether it was betrayal or some other painful situation, Troy, like a lot of men, just kept moving on. "I'm fine, I'm fine."

In a way, I admired that because it was so different from me and seemed so strong. But I had relied on his system working, and we were entering a season where so much was piled on us that any weakness was going to be fully exposed. Until you experience enough pain, I've concluded, you deny that it's actually there.

FIGHTING BATTLES FOR HIM

As he fought, or at least ignored, his internal battles, Troy seemed increasingly distant and checked-out. His goal was always to get off the medication—which he regarded as a scarlet letter. He was convinced that with diet and exercise alone, he could tear that scarlet "M" off and conquer the attacks that had exposed his vulnerability.

The practical result was that I was doing as much as I could to lead the church and take things off his plate. At executive-team meetings, Troy often looked like a deer in the headlights or antsy or distracted. He would go to the bathroom three times, and sit there checking his phone. When someone would say, "Can we do this?" his usual reply was, "Just run with it."

Later, I would say, "Troy, we can't just run with everything." But he didn't take it too seriously, and he told me not to worry so much.

Is this the medication talking? I wondered. *What's going on here?*

Fearing that his problem was creating a leadership vacuum, I began to play a greater role. It was an incredibly busy time for Freedom House. We were opening new campuses and developing a teaching team, and I was preaching a lot on the weekends. During the week, I led our executive-team meetings. When Troy was present, I shoved papers into his hands, briefed him quickly, and pushed him into the room hoping he could pull it off. Maybe he thought the church was running itself, but I was feeling the heavy weight of not letting things collapse.

I was very careful when making decisions to keep Troy in the position of honor and authority. I always used language like, "Pastor Troy and I decided," and, "Let me talk to Pastor Troy and get back to you," even when I knew in advance what the answer would be. When I came up with titles for message series and made creative decisions, I had Troy rubber-stamp them and then told the teams, "Troy came up with really good things, and I did, too."

I actually became fearful that if I wasn't involved in a decision, he might make a bad one. An unwelcome hyper-vigilance came over me.

One time a high-profile visiting leader came to speak at our church and saw how I ran the services. Afterward he said, "I don't see many women who can run stuff the way you just ran everything." That didn't make me feel good—It made me feel nervous. I was already coming to building meetings and construction sites to make decisions with all the guys there. I was concerned about how I was coming across and if I seemed to be overshadowing Troy, so I did things like bake cookies for the workers to communicate that I was still a "girl," while at the same time telling them that certain things were unacceptable and this and that needed to be fixed or rebuilt.

I was dumbing myself down to make my husband look in-charge as we fought this battle.

There was no denying it: My personality turned into Ft. Knox, just to push things through. I'm very much a woman submitted to authority, not an "I am woman, hear me roar" type. But I felt pressed on all sides trying to hold our lives together, and I couldn't afford a lot of extraneous conversation. I often got edgy with our staff members and went into commander mode, firing off short text messages: "Do this. Do that. This hasn't happened." To the high-feelers on our staff, and there are many, I came across as harsh, mean, and insensitive. Gone were the days I would take a moment to ask, "Hey, how are you feeling today?" I just didn't have the time or energy for niceties.

Am I a Jezebel? A horrible person? I wondered many times while tapping out orders and directives. *I am not cool with what I have become.*

During this time, Troy was exercising and pampering himself so much that I had to make him spend more time at the office. He came across almost like a figurehead at times.

"I'm going home to study," or, "I'm going to the gym," he would say.

"Troy, your face needs to be here," I told him with the door closed. "Stay in your office and study. Leadership is managing expectations. You cannot announce at two o'clock that you're going to the gym and not coming back. And, by the way, you can't post pictures of you on the golf course anymore."

I was his public relations manager as well.

Interestingly, Troy served very effectively at other churches and in certain settings, like when teaching teams or small groups. But if he had to speak to a large group on a big platform or with people in attendance who had a lot of influence, I would see him freaking out.

"Babe, you do this all the time," I reassured him more than once. "You'll get up and do your best. You've done this message before."

Then he would start acting funny and say, "Y'all go out. I'm gonna go to the bathroom." I remember standing in a worship service at a church of 20,000 people thinking, *Is he really going to come out? What will happen if he doesn't?*

Back in Charlotte, I would see him on Sunday mornings reach into our bathroom cabinet, pull out a Xanax, and slip it into his pocket. I started counting the pills left in the bottle. He kept the Xanax in his pocket but would not take his daily pills. He was convinced he didn't need them.

I learned to recognize the small symptoms signaling an oncoming attack. Troy gets up at 5 a.m. on Sundays to go through his message. I would hear him clearing his throat and know that his throat was tightening. A panic attack had begun. As he prayed, the throat clearing would become constant.

Don't ask him about it, I would tell myself. *It'll only send him farther into it.*

Yes, but if I don't, something really bad might happen today, and I will be responsible, another voice said.

By now Troy would be coughing and almost gagging, which is how an attack progressed. The stress of that happening Sunday after Sunday was overwhelming. If I took the risk and asked him through the bathroom door, "Hey, what's going on?" he would reply, "Nothing. Everything's good."

At church, he sometimes fogged out and seemed to lose his way while preaching.

"Are you okay?" I asked afterward on some occasions.

He always made it sound like I was trying to talk down his abilities.

"I know I'm not a good enough preacher for you," he'd say. "I know you're disappointed."

Exactly the opposite, I thought. *You're my favorite preacher. You just kind of blanked out up there, and I'm trying to figure out what's going on.*

After a while, especially when he tried to get off his daily medication on his own, I was afraid to hear Troy preach. I sat on the front row, squeezing my hands together, praying for a good outcome. I went to every service he spoke in, and when he asked why I was always there, I said, "Oh, I just wanted to be with you." But really I wanted to be there in case he couldn't continue, and someone had to jump up and cover for him.

Sometimes the worst happened and Troy went into a full panic attack—gagging, sweating, eyes darting, breaths coming quickly—and someone else, often I, had to step in. Walking through that in such a way that simultaneously comforted and covered him felt almost impossible. Then the work week would start, and I was pulling long days at the church, raising up others to lead, and leading our executive team during what should have been the most exciting time for our church. Few people knew of Troy's panic attacks, so we lacked the support that we sorely needed.

God, I know you wired me to be a strong woman, I prayed, *but I'm doing so much, and I don't think this is an isolated season anymore. This is our new life. I'm trapped by Troy's issue and constantly filling in, fixing, covering. Where does it all end?*

SELF-TREATING

Meanwhile, Troy was living the good life, from my perspective. He dedicated himself to CrossFit, to relaxing—which often meant golf—to a healthy diet, even to entertainment. The doctor had given him a list of 25 things to help avoid panic attacks—things like "Don't send emails" and "Watch something light and funny"—and Troy was doing them diligently. At home, after he had been at the gym and I at the church, he would lay in bed and laugh hysterically at late night talk shows, because that was on the list. Fury would build up in me as I thought, *Glad one of us can laugh. You enjoy your little CrossFit routine and funny shows and healthy diet, and I'll keep our ministry lives going. How about that?*

If I mentioned that I was feeling under the gun and needed help, Troy inevitably told me something like, "Why are you so stressed? Let stuff roll off you." He scolded me for bringing work home.

"Put the computer down. Relax a little," he said. "You're working too much."

I thought, *I feel like you've dumped everything on me. You're supposed to be covering me, and I'm covering you! I don't mind doing that for a season, but it's not my permanent role.*

If I mentioned this openly, Troy's response was hostile: "You're seeing this all wrong. I'm fine."

His easygoing demeanor meant that our kids didn't see a lot of negativity from him in that season. In fact, he came across as the fun parent. Every day was a play day to Troy, and I was the bad guy enforcing rules. Before the panic attacks, he would glance at what our girls were wearing before they left the house and tell them, "You go change that." Now one of our daughters would come home, and I would look at her and ask, "Your dad took you to school today in that?" "Yeah," she would say. Stuff that used to get checked at the door wasn't getting checked. When I laid down the law and marched her up to pick out something else to wear, she got mad at me, even if Troy told her I was right.

What scared me the most was that my husband was no longer dreaming about the church or ministry, which had always been our shared passion. His new goals were things like, "I want to qualify for the Charlotte Amateur or the CrossFit Games." I wanted to say, "Where's the church dreaming? I'd love you to be as passionate about what's going on at Freedom House as you are about golf and CrossFit. We used to lay our heads on our pillows at night and dream about the church we now have. How about setting goals for us there? How about getting excited about that again?"

Robotically, I pressed through, not wanting to consider what I had become as a result of what had happened to Troy. In the back of my mind, the questions always hovered:

Is this the new Troy?
What happened to the guy I married?
What good is a pastor who can't preach?
How long can I keep carrying things and covering what's happening?
Is this the end of it all? Is everything we dreamed of slipping away?

CHAPTER 6
FORCING THE CONVERSATION

The situation hit an all-time low for me (Penny) with some issues that happened on our team. One of the things we learned from our friend John Maxwell is that when a church gets to a certain size there are three issues you always have to deal with: STAFF, STAFF, and STAFF. We went through a very tough season of staff issues. We were going through some tough hires and some tough fires that needed to be dealt with.

These problems arose when Troy was spending less time focused on leadership stuff and more on getting well. As conflict and disagreement increased on our staff, I asked myself, *Do we have some tares in our field that need to be dealt with?* Jesus talked about how when men were sleeping, the enemy came and sowed tares—weeds—in the field. It felt to me like Troy was sleeping, and the enemy was sowing weeds in our wheat field.

I knew from studying Jesus' parable that the only way to know the difference between wheat and tares was to wait and see what fruit they ultimately produced. A tare mimics wheat, and Jesus said to let both grow up, so you could differentiate them in later stages. Pulling them out—firing prematurely— would cause sure disruption on our staff, especially among those hired to support in certain departments. I needed time for things to grow, and I needed great discernment.

I also needed Troy to engage with what was going on.

"We have problems that need to be addressed," I started telling him.

Troy relied a lot on my gift of discernment, but like any good boss he didn't want to jump to conclusions and fire someone quickly. He preferred we lie back and give as much grace as we could. However, because I was the one dealing with day-to-day things, I saw the damage a few toxic staff were causing up close. I began to feel under siege, like everything was a strategic chess move, and sometimes I just wanted to play checkers—simply jump the man and take him without having to analyze everything.

I prayed—hard.

Lord, I need you to be very specific with us about what to do. When we let people go, there are children involved, spouses who did nothing. We are pastors, and we want to know if there is any part of this that we can redeem? Any part that's an emotional allergy on our part from a previous hurt? Please be super-clear about what to do.

Clarity came with the worsening behavior. One signed important contracts we had told him not to. The other became belligerent—to the point of dysfunction—toward our leadership. Because I didn't feel that Troy and I could sit down and make the final decision together, or that my word would be enough to convince Troy to wield the ax, I took the path of building a case to present to Troy. With his permission, I invited a business coach to assess our staff and, I hoped, pull back the curtains on our in-house enemies. That's exactly what happened.

"You have a great staff," the coach reported back to us, "except for a couple of team members who are just not with you. They are just not a fit for the church staff."

With that diagnosis, Troy fired the instigators, and some other people quit out of loyalty to them. It was disruptive on a corporate and a personal level, but as soon as they were gone, peace was restored to our team. The tares disappeared from among us. I wasn't walking around with a magnifying glass, afraid of what I would discover.

In their place, God gave us amazing new team members, both of whom share our hearts and are experts in their fields. It was like God said, "I know you've been through a lot; let me give you a couple of fantastic people."

But the fight had taken its toll on me.

CONFRONTATION

I finally decided I was done with Troy's "I'm fine." Done with the doctor's 25 things. Done pulling more weight than I felt I should. Done acting like medication was evil and that Troy was okay. I wanted to be honoring, but I started bringing up my concerns in pointed ways.

"Troy, I feel like I'm carrying a lot of weight at the church," I told him. "I'm strong, but not that strong. I need you to check back in and start handling some of this stuff."

"Things are going great," he said. "Maybe you're not see-ing it right."

"Things are going great because I'm working my butt off,"

I said. "You've got to get healthy enough to get back in the game with me."

"I'm fine," he said.

"Your 'fine' is causing me stress," I said. "You're denying there's an issue, and I'm taking on your stuff and my stuff. A season of downtime is one thing, but when I can't see the light at the end of the tunnel, it's gone on long enough."

"I just don't see it that way," he said. "Things are really good right now."

Dude, I'm counting your anxiety pills. Things are not really good, I thought. *I know you're taking Xanax.*

"Listen, I don't want to take your man-card from you, but I keep reading online that panic attacks can be controlled with medication, and I think you should do that again," I said.

I might as well have said that I considered him a failure.

"I don't need daily medication. I'm fine," he answered.

"You're not. I've been pulling your weight for a long time," I said bluntly. "You're an ostrich with your head in the sand, and I need you to pull it out."

He didn't like arguing with me because my upbringing taught me to argue until I won, so he started bringing up his problem when other people were around so that I had to limit what I said. Back home, when it was just the two of us, if I brought the difficult subject up again he'd say, "We already discussed that."

"No, we didn't," I'd say. "You brought it up when other people were around because you knew I wouldn't release the Kraken. You are not going to play this passive game and try to sweep this conversation under the rug knowing I won't dishonor you in other people's presence."

More often than not, he would just be silent. The sense of vulnerability was almost palpable.

"Troy, this isn't healthy," I said gently but firmly. "You're hiding. You're avoiding. Please look into going back on daily medication until we get some other answer. I love you; however, I want the person I know you are, the man I married, the man I dreamt with."

TELLING THE BOARD

Troy and I have always been people of accountability, so I decided to "call an audible" and make us accountable to our pastors and our board. Even then, I feared deeply that they would think I was a Jezebel, somehow trying to control Troy. But I could think of no other path, so I opened the conversation about how I felt, what I was seeing, what had happened with the two toxic team members, and more.

"I need y'all's help," was my basic message. "I feel trapped in a catch-22. Troy is still having panic attacks, and he's hiding it from me. I don't know what to do."

I was totally surprised when one board member said, "Penny, I had panic attacks and hid it from my wife, too. I never wanted to not be "the man" in her eyes. When you have a panic attack you feel weak, flawed, and damaged which are the last things you want to feel in front of your wife. The shame is so intense."

71

Those words inspired something I hadn't felt for a while: compassion for Troy.

What would I feel like if I were paralyzed by fear? I wondered. *What must that feel like for him?*

As I put on Troy's shoes, my anger started to subside. I felt safe telling Troy that I had called the board because I was struggling, and they began to have conversations that were supportive and healthy. Because they were men who had faced similar challenges, Troy felt they identified with him in ways that I could not.

I also talked with a doctor friend of ours, Dr. Robi. He teaches at churches about how the brain is wired and illuminates the spiritual realities in addition to the medical perspective.

"Can you talk to Troy?" I asked him while he was teaching at our church. "I think he should be on medication, and he won't do it."

Dr. Robi followed up with him, and a month or so later, Troy started a new kind of conversation with me.

"Hey, I was talking to Dr. Robi about whether I should be on daily medication," he said. "I think I'm going to talk to my doctor about it again."

"That's great," I said with a level tone. Inside, I was doing cartwheels. At the time he would only take reactive medication, not proactive medication.

After his visit to the doctor, Troy's entire perspective

changed. The doctor had told him that most people he saw in high-level positions—those running companies and large organizations—took medication. He didn't know why Troy was beating himself up about it.

"This type of thing is not uncommon," the doctor said, according to Troy. "There's a lot coming your way, and it's not easy to process. Almost all CEOs and leaders take something because there's so much on their shoulders."

Troy's whole perspective changed.

"Penny, it's not just me," he said.

Truth had won out. Troy wasn't broken. He was a normal human being doing extraordinary things.

But for me, getting back to normal took a little longer.

THE WELL OF ANGER

Troy got back to form and had increasing energy for our church, our relationship, and our vision for the future. It was a huge relief. But my healing journey had just begun. Two years earlier, we had unwisely stopped meeting with our counselor because Troy figured his therapy was in the gym or on the golf course. We now agreed to resume meeting with him, this time by video conference, because he was in Atlanta.

In our home office, Troy and I sat for counseling sessions in front of our computer. It was good to connect with our long-time counselor and life coach again. Within a short amount of time, to my surprise, Troy was talking about how he had quit dreaming about ministry things because church matters could set off panic attacks, while the golf course and gym were safe. He naturally wanted to stick with things that didn't trigger him.

Troy had essentially built himself a panic room that he could run to in order to be safe. The downside was that inside a panic room, you are stuck. Life is limited. You're mostly alone. You have to continually do things like golf or work out just to stay in that space. It gets selfish very quickly.

"Troy, that self-protective response served a purpose when you were a kid and all that bad stuff was happening in your life," the counselor said. "Now it's time to thank that defense mechanism and let it go. You're not in that harmful environment anymore. You don't need to manifest the same way of dealing with things."

Then the counselor turned to me. I was feeling pretty justified. I didn't have a panic room. I was the one holding things together. Or so I thought.

"Penny, I've been counseling you and Troy for fifteen years, and not one time have you ever blamed God for anything in your life—your sexual abuse, physical abuse, emotional abuse," the counselor said. "I have never seen you blame God."

Yes, knowing it wasn't God's fault is the only thing that got me through, I thought as I enjoyed the praise and recognition.

"You have never played the victim—until now," the counselor continued.

Major record scratch.

What?! I thought.

He went on.

"In this situation, you're acting like a victim," he said. "You are blaming Troy for the weight you're under. I want to call that to your attention because I have never seen you do this before."

Without any warning, I exploded with anger.

"Because it's his fault!" I yelled at the screen, pointing at Troy. "Because he won't acknowledge what he's done. Because I won't feel safe until he knows what he did to me. Because this is the person I'm supposed to be intimate with spiritually, physically, emotionally, every way. But I can't trust him until he sees how I feel."

Unexpectedly, I began to think of my dad, who had died of alcoholism. I had learned to identify safe and unsafe people and to disengage from relationships where there was no acknowledgment of what was broken. If someone can't see the damage they do, there's no hope for real relationship or safety—or change. I had placed Troy into that unsafe category.

My heart beat faster, and I pulled in deep, rapid breaths—not unlike Troy in his panic attacks. I felt suddenly out of control when I had held everything in control for so long.

"Tell me, why all the anger?" the counselor asked.

I became furious with him.

"Oh, I know what you're doing now," I said. "I counsel

people enough. I know anger is not a primary emotion; it's a secondary emotion and is present when there's an unresolved hurt. You're trying to tap into my unresolved hurt. I'll be honest with y'all: anger feels much more powerful than hurting and waving a white flag around like I'm some wounded bird. With anger I can slam my hand down on the desk and protect myself. But if I break down and cry, then I have to admit I'm weak in front of him. And I don't trust him with my weakness right now."

I knew I was exposing myself as I talked, and I desperately wished the counselor would cut in and stop me.

"I know what you're fishing for!" I continued. "You're trying to get to my belief systems. The more I talk the more you'll find out what they are. Let me tell you, belief systems are BS. That's right! This is all BS."

For a moment our little room was quiet. I had stumbled onto an area that was off-limits in my own heart. An area where hurt poured out uncontrolled, and I couldn't harness my tongue. It was the one area I kept locked away. For the first time in my life, I had bottled something up—blaming others and giving them the key to my life.

I had built my own panic room.

"I'm going to suggest we hold separate sessions for a while," the counselor said. "Troy, your wife is going to have to get some of this out because she's been stacking for a long time, and there are layers of hurt there."

Troy nodded. He seemed as surprised as I was by what had just burst out of me.

MAXWELL VS. MAXWELL

I had never pulled my heart or physical relationship back from Troy during the difficult season, but bottling the blame had turned me into a volatile partner—like a volcano threatening to blow.

One aspect of the journey that had wounded me was when Troy began to step back into more active leadership again. I was relieved as I saw him lead well, and I learned to trust him with decision-making and preaching and other things. But as he regained his confidence, it felt like we were competitors for a while, like having two chiefs in the same room. In a way, it felt like he needed to oust me from authority. Sometimes he made jabs and comments at me in meetings, as if putting me in my place. Sometimes he publicly overruled decisions I had made and said, "Well, I didn't tell you to do that."

I did it because you weren't here to do it! I felt like screaming, but I didn't.

A number of times I felt demeaned, dismissed, and flatout dissed in front of people. Here I had been feeding Troy the ball for years so he could make easy baskets and remain the respected leader, and now when I went for a layup, he knocked my feet out from under me. It felt like someone trying to transfer his shame to me. Not only that, he disregarded all the points I had put on the board while he was on the bench.

I told him straight up, when we were alone: "Babe, you can't come back in here and act like the big man on campus by competing with me all the time. It feels like there's an invisible scoreboard, and you're trying to put points up. I don't want to be your competitor."

"That's foolishness," he replied. "I'm not competing with you."

"It's not foolishness," I said. "When you're feeling insecure, you become my competitor. I don't want you picking at me like that anymore."

My anger at what I perceived as his ingratitude and unkindness came boiling over in our counseling meetings.

"You hung me out to dry," I told Troy as our counselor looked on. "You felt like a failure and turned on me out of insecurity. I've been running the show, and there were things you did not even know about. Now you want to grab it back and smack me on the hand? Dude, this is the last way you should be treating me! I should be the Queen of Sheba to you right now. You should be peeling my grapes and feeding them to me. I don't know many pastors' wives who could have done what I did. You should be kissing my doggone feet and saying, 'Babe, where would I be without you?'"

It felt good to say. And Troy was good about owning up to things. I vividly remember the day the panic room door finally opened, and he talked about what was going on inside.

"It's like when you hurt your leg and don't want people to get too close," he said. "I treated life like that because I didn't want to put too much pressure on myself. I was shirking some responsibilities because I wanted to get well, to get back in the game. I was exercising a lot, playing a lot of golf because everything was foggy. I was preaching but not making a lot of decisions, not going to the office much, not leading the staff well because it was hard to. I was putting so much energy into not having a panic attack. Eighty percent of my time was in my head trying to avoid all situations that could be a trigger."

As I listened, relief washed over me.

"I've been struggling with concentration," he continued. "I wanted to get off the medication so badly that I made that my one goal. In the process, I left it all on her. I'm sorry about that, Penny."

Deep peace came into my soul for the first time in a long time. The acknowledgment of my pain probably meant as much to me as my recognition of his pain meant to him. It also assured me that I hadn't been out of my mind.

"You know, I used to think that nothing ever fazed you, that you were Superman," I told my husband, whom I loved. "Now I'm realizing that being Superman is not healthy. Kryptonite always finds its way in when we don't learn to process what happens. Nobody comes through all their experiences unscathed. They leave a mark."

We had both come to a profound and unexpected discovery: When you're hurting, the most important thing is not to run into the panic room. It's the last place you want to be.

CHAPTER 7
WORKING TOGETHER AGAIN

It took me a while to realize how much weight I had put on Penny and to see the depth of her feelings about what we were walking through. In my mind I was still hitting important marks—being present at the office, preaching four times a week, getting emotionally healthier—but running things day-to-day at the church had taken a greater toll on Penny than I had known. I felt really bad when it became clear what I had done to her. But instead of feeling crushing disappointment or failure, I was somewhat energized by the fact that we had identified the mess, and now I had the opportunity to help clean it up.

Penny and I had long ago established healthy rules of engagement for our arguments:

- No yelling, because yelling is an attempt to control.
- No silent treatment. One of us might need to take a break every now and then, but we did not allow ourselves to walk around the house for five days not talking.
- No bringing up resolved issues.
- No using derogatory or unkind words.
- Listen. Don't just wait to talk.
- Don't react.
- Disagree with dignity.
- Aim for a good result. Build a bridge; don't burn it down.

These are good principles for every married couple, and I encourage husbands and wives to come up with healthy rules of engagement like these. Fighting fair often means changing weapons from the hurtful ones we are accustomed to wielding. Love doesn't tear down and try to dominate. Love is the great bridge-builder. It says in Ephesians 5:2 (NKJV):

And walk in love, as Christ also has loved us and given Himself for us, an offering and a sacrifice to God for a sweet-smelling aroma.

We all want that sweet-smelling aroma in our marriages, not the acrid odor of unresolved conflict. And yet somehow, in the midst of building a fast-growing church, we had encountered a problem that went beyond our rules. It demanded new, more proactive responses to keep the love flowing in our marriage. Panic attacks exposed weaknesses in our relationship that we didn't know were there. Panic attacks caused breakdowns in communication that needed addressing.

IMBALANCE IN OUR MARRIAGE

One of my problems was that I valued Penny's opinion of me so highly that I could not handle negative feedback from her. One time in counseling, our life coach asked me point-blank, "Why do you give Penny so much power in your life?"

I had never thought of it that way.

"I put a lot of emphasis on what she thinks about me because I'm her husband and a leader," I tried to answer. "I respect her. Her opinion matters to me."

"But you're putting her in an unhealthy place," he responded. "When you give someone that much power, that person becomes your god. You end up doing whatever you do for her approval."

He was shining a light in a difficult place. I gave so much weight to Penny's words that I took everything personally, even when she was trying to help me. For example, I couldn't really receive criticism about my preaching from her. It made me feel betrayed, rejected, and dishonored. That in turn fueled a competitive impulse in me to try to win her respect by being right, or looking good in front of others, or winning arguments. Let me tell you, winning an argument with Penny is a tough thing to do because she's great at making her case, and she won't quit. Put us in front of a staff member or two and an argument turned into a measure of my value (in my previous, broken way of thinking), and I would fight hard to win. Penny and I would both end up feeling wounded, dishonored, and unappreciated.

"You two are going to have differences of opinion," our life coach assured us. "Troy, you have to be okay with that. You have to make it safe. Different opinions are not rejection. You don't have to let them eat at you. You can both walk away from an argument without winning it, and you can still honor and support each other."

Of course, for strong personalities, the temptation is to fight until only one of you is left standing. But that wasn't working for our relationship. I began to trust God—not Penny—with my self-image. He had called me and given me the assignment to preach and lead, so what ultimately mattered was His approval, not anyone else's. That allowed me to hear what Penny had to say, wherever that fell on the scale of praise and criticism. I actually started to take her criticisms to heart in a positive way, and to grow from them.

That, in itself, was a minor miracle and a big step forward.

This shift was not an easy journey. It took a lot of reflection, time in prayer, and vulnerability. I spent time with some of my good friends who assured me of my worth. When you go through something that debilitates, it's so easy to feel unworthy and devalued. Sometimes you just need some people who can speak into your potential.

Shifting my thinking so that God's opinion mattered most, and allowing myself to receive praise from Him was huge.

NO PLACE FOR SHAME

I also discovered that while the physiological reasons for panic attacks were relatively easy to treat, the underlying emotional reasons were harder to remedy. For me, and I think a lot of people, shame had long been a battle. The shadow of shame first fell on people in the perfect garden when Adam and Eve actually tried to hide from God rather than be seen in their shame. Interestingly, God already had a plan to cover their nakedness and shame—the first act of grace toward humanity. But Adam and Eve didn't see it that way.

> Then the LORD God called to Adam and said to him, "Where are you?" So he said, "I heard Your voice in the garden, and I was afraid because I was naked; and I hid myself." —Genesis 3:9, 10 (NKJV)

Fear became their primary emotion and hiding their shame their primary motivation. Fear causes shame. The acronym I have always heard for FEAR is False Evidence Appearing Real. When we have a thought, it becomes a picture or image. That image becomes a habit. Then fear becomes a habit.

Shame can easily be the thing that hides that habit. Shame, at its core, is feeling wrong about who you are. It's very different from guilt which comes from doing something wrong. Shame causes a person to think, *There is something wrong with me. I am defective in some way.* Adam and Eve had no experience with God's mercy even though they knew His goodness. That same reaction has been passed on to every human being since. When we battle shame, we don't give ourselves any room for God's grace. Instead, we run away from the help that we need. We end up hiding just like Adam and Eve. Shame becomes the bush we hide behind.

Psalm 34:5 (NLT) says, "Those who look to him for help will be radiant with joy; no shadow of shame will darken their faces." Living in shame is selfish because it means our eyes are on our problems and not on God's solutions. We devalue and dishonor grace when we allow shame to govern our emotions, thoughts, actions, and words.

I speak as one who has lived that way. I used to beat myself up, blaming myself for my mess, for living beneath the story God was writing about me. Instead of looking "to him for help" as the Psalm says, I focused on my failures. So my face was darkened with shame, and I was not radiant with joy. Rather, I was trying to defeat a problem that only God's grace could defeat in me. God never judges us based on our humanity. If He did, no one would survive the audit. Rather, He judges us based on our surrender to His grace. That is why Paul could write,

So now there is no condemnation for those who belong to Christ Jesus. —Romans 8:1 (NLT)

Condemnation is the opposite of grace. Grace frees us from shame and condemnation. It is empowered by what God did, not what we do. Grace looks like Jesus! Our part is to have the courage to trust Him. Grace means accepting that we can't do it alone. Grace covers our failure and ensures our success. God is amazing that way—He's full of grace.

And the Word became flesh and dwelt among us, and we beheld His glory, the glory as of the only begotten of the Father, full of grace and truth. —John 1:14 (NKJV)

WOUNDS FROM THE PAST

A lot of my shame stemmed from situations in my childhood. In an effort to encourage and instruct me when I lived with my grandparents, my paternal grandmother would compare me to other kids. "Jimmy is doing this. Why don't you do this?" As great a woman as she was, my grandmother was also, in those days, the queen of the guilt-trip. She was extremely good at using guilt to prod you in certain directions. I still remember the power of her sad expression and her disappointed eyes to get me to do what she wanted. I don't blame her for it now. It was just a lever she pulled to try to guide me in the right way. But it instilled in me a shame-based action system that made it hard to accept criticism or disappointment from those around me.

I was also ashamed of my dad. In college, I tried to have a relationship with him. He would party with me all the time, and everybody loved him, but it was embarrassing to watch his cycle of getting wasted and passing out, then starting all over again. He began traveling at some point, and I met the Lord. When he called to get together because he was back in town, I would tell him bluntly, "Dad, you're an alcoholic. I don't want to see you."

"I quit drinking," was his standard reply.

As a new Christian I felt mercy and compassion for him, but my attempts to have a real relationship not based on substance abuse always failed. And because I had a propensity for drinking, I didn't want to go anywhere near his lifestyle.

When Penny and I got married, I invited Dad to the wedding but told him, "I don't want you acting like a goofball and ruining this for us." Of course he didn't listen. He made a scene, hitting on the bridesmaids, and showed up drunk.

The last time he saw my children was on Colby and Cabell's birthday. (They were born on the same day, two years apart.) He showed up drunk to their party. I think Cabell was just one year old, and Colby was three. After that, I put distance between us. I had to set up some serious boundaries. He never met his youngest grandchild, Cassidy.

Even through all of this, I knew my dad was a great guy—when he wasn't drinking. He had a disease called alcoholism, and the traumatic head injury had made it worse.

He died when I was in Dallas, Texas, at a pastors' conference. Dad was living in Boca Raton, Florida. He had developed leukemia. His life ended alone in a bare little apartment. Penny was with me in that hotel room in Dallas when the news came. I started crying.

"I don't even know why I'm crying, or why I'm upset about it," I said. I thought I had walked away from that relationship and all the baggage that went with it.

A friend of mine from Canada was at the conference with me, and I confided in him.

"My dad never did anything worth anything," I told him. "He wasted his entire life."

This guy literally grabbed me. He said, "Listen, Troy, don't say that. He made one good thing, and that was you."

Those words helped me immensely to appreciate my dad's life and to deal with his sad death. It helped me understand why the Bible is so emphatic about honoring the generations that come before us. In honoring them, we are honoring ourselves. We are affirming the value of our own lives because our parents and grandparents gave us life. That's a huge deal that outweighs pretty much everything negative they might do.

I went alone to clean out Dad's apartment. There was virtually nothing there besides a mattress, a metal folding chair, and a last will and testament, unless you count all the Scotch bottles. Not even a TV or a table. I read his will and, true to form, he wanted an extravagant celebration service in memorial. He had no money, but he wanted Ron Moody and the Centaurs to come play at the ritzy Belmont Golf Course to celebrate his life with a bunch of guests. He had even written the amounts of money to pay various people for participating. That celebration idea was Dad's last pipe-dream and endearing in its own way. I had his body cremated, and some of his friends sprinkled his ashes in the ocean because Dad loved the beach.

That same year, Dad's mother died, and her life stood in stark contrast to his, at least in our family's experience. I had moved her to Charlotte to be near us after my grandfather passed away. She became an important part of my kids' lives, and they loved her. She sat on the front row of our church and always said I was her favorite preacher. She was so kind and loving to us. She had made Penny's wedding dress and given us great recipes that we use to this day. Her legacy in our family remains strong.

When I read in the Bible about the great cloud of witnesses, I always think of my grandmother sitting in the bleachers cheering me on. It is one of the happier thoughts from my past.

I don't think we realize the effects the past has on the present in our lives—especially if we don't ever deal with them, talk about them, or simply process them. For me, the weight of all that definitely had something to do with the pot that had come to a boil in my emotional life. It had been covered for so long, and now it was bubbling over.

EMOTIONS ARE YOUR FRIEND

Revisiting a lot of negative memories about my dad in counseling clued me in to the fact that I was ignoring some intense emotions. I learned the hard way that we are emotional beings. We can't ignore or suppress our emotions. In my case, I had a problem simply being aware of my emotions and identifying what was going on inside of me. Like other men, I'm sure, I prefer to push emotions away rather than discern them and appreciate what they are telling me. Given the option, I didn't want to feel. But not acknowledging my emotions didn't protect me; it ended up hurting me.

Emotions are the barometer of the spirit in a man. They tell you what's going on in your soul. Emotions are neither bad nor good. They are there to tell you what's happening inside of you. They are an internal health indicator, but they should never be a life driver. A lot of people are driven by emotions, and that's just as unhealthy as ignoring them. Emotions can take you down plenty of bad paths if you try to satisfy or justify them rather than live by faith and the Word of God. Hebrews 10:38 (KJV) tells us, "Now the just shall live by faith." Faith and the proper management of our emotional lives help us lead God-inspired, God-led lives of meaning and purpose.

Taking a hard look at my emotions, I saw that I wasn't being honest with myself, God, and others about the stress that I felt of growing a church. I wasn't stewarding my soul the way God created me to do. By running from pain, I missed its lesson. Pain is your friend. When you have an abscessed tooth or an ulcer, you feel pain. That pain is an indicator that you need to repair a problem. You need to give it your attention. If you don't, infection can spread throughout your entire body. If you listen to pain signals and act on them, your body can avoid infection.

Panic attacks were not my root issue but the result of ignoring indicators I should have been paying attention to. Infection spread through my soul as the enemy used my "failure" to eat away at my self-confidence and passion for my God-given assignments. Philippians 4:6-7 (NKJV) and Colossians 3:15 (NKJV) became key verses for me on which to build my emotional life. Respectively, they say:

Be anxious for nothing, but in everything by prayer and supplication, with thanksgiving, let your requests be made known to God; and the peace of God, which surpasses all understanding, will guard your hearts and minds through Christ Jesus.

And let the peace of God rule in your hearts, to which also you were called in one body; and be thankful.

The peace of God is an amazing reality. It means nothing is missing, nothing is broken, nothing is scattered. Peace means being complete and whole. It does not, however, mean the absence of storms. Rather, God's peace is internal and allows us to live in the greatest of storms and still be calm. It is a state of the soul rather than an external condition.

God's peace "surpasses all understanding"; it is beyond our emotional and intellectual apprehension. It is a product of faith. This peace "will guard your hearts and minds." It sets up a barrier between our circumstances and our hearts and minds. It becomes an advocate for our emotional stability. It sets up a guard—a strong military term—around our souls.

It then goes beyond that to "rule in your hearts." Peace becomes our decision-maker! It becomes our guide. The godly life is led by peace. It directs us through life.

Each of us has a need for this prevailing peace in our hearts and minds. Jesus recognized this when He healed the woman with the issue of blood. Read His response carefully:

And He said to her, "Daughter, your faith has made you well, go in peace, and be healed of your affliction." —Mark 5:34 (NKJV)

The peace the woman needed was in addition to the healing she needed. Jesus healed her physical pain and her emotional pain. She had suffered with her physical problem for years, and the emotional toll was significant. So, Jesus gave her the gift of peace.

Jesus cares about our whole being—body, soul, and spirit—and gives us the peace to overcome toxic emotions. I'm convinced now that to really receive His peace, we have to know that we need it. We have to recognize our emotional condition and need. That was a powerful lesson that panic attacks helped me to appreciate.

MY MESSY LIFE

Any shame I continued to feel about having a messy life was wiped away by seeing how messy the lives of Bible people were. Being messy was almost a prerequisite to being greatly used! Think of any hero of the faith, and you'll find that in some way he or she was a mess. Adam and Eve were a mess and caused a mess for billions of people. Abraham and Sarah were a mess, but Abraham is still the father of faith. Joseph messed up, as did his father Jacob, and the righteous preacher Noah, Elijah the prophet, Peter the chief apostle, and on down the line. All exhibited glaring weaknesses and had messy lives.

The underlying secret is this: One small crack doesn't mean you are broken. It means you were put to the test and didn't fall apart. God will still do awesome things through you. Don't let the enemy use your perceived failures to disqualify you from greatness.

God uses messy people because that's the only kind of people available.

Elijah's story especially speaks to me because, like him, I have experienced public success followed by emotional pain. Elijah won some crazy battles, and yet often after great victory, people feel the most alone and the most vulnerable. After one of the greatest days in all the Bible, after defeating hundreds of prophets of Baal by calling fire from heaven, it says of Elijah,

Then he went on alone into the wilderness, traveling all day. He sat down under a solitary broom tree and prayed that he might die. "I have had enough, LORD," he said. "Take my life, for I am no better than my ancestors who have already died." —1 Kings 19:4 (NLT)

The wilderness speaks of the place where we have to deal with our personal demons. Jesus faced the devil in the wilderness. The Israelites spent forty years in the wilderness. Often the length of time in the wilderness is equal to the amount of time it takes to purge our past hurts, betrayals, identity crises, and so on.

I picture Elijah, one of the greatest prophets in the Bible, in this depressed moment. Alone in the wilderness, under what the Bible so pointedly calls a "solitary broom tree," he went so far as to pray that he might die! This was an act of spiritual suicide by a hero of the faith. Though I have never been suicidal, I can identify with that. It seems to me that Elijah wanted to commit self-sabotage for the purpose of hiding his weakness. I, too, was so afraid of looking weak to my wife and others that death seemed preferable—and my brain interpreted this fear as an actual threat which caused panic attacks.

I had to learn that God isn't afraid of my mess. In fact, God is attracted to my mess. Jesus chose to hang around with messy people.

The religion scholars and Pharisees saw him keeping this kind of company and lit into his disciples: "What kind of example is this, acting cozy with the riffraff?" Jesus, overhearing, shot back, "Who needs a doctor: the healthy or the sick? I'm here inviting the sin-sick, not the spiritually-fit." —Mark 2:16–17 (The Message)

This sheds light on a priceless principle: *The depth of my honesty invites the greatness of God's presence.* Jesus did not like being with people who denied their messes. He embraced those who were publicly messy. I can't tell you how encouraging that is for me—and for all of us.

Not until we come to grips with our weakness and mess does God's grace become sufficient (2 Corinthians 12:9). If you are stuck in a messy life, this truth just might save your ministry, your marriage, and your very life. Run to God with your mess and quit hiding it. He will reveal who you are and what's really going on inside of you all, so that He can heal you and give you His peace.

Penny's and my life-coach sessions were really good about revealing my messes and reintroducing me to my emotions, giving them proper honor and value. They helped with building on areas where I was weakest, like having empathy. I learned to quit ignoring or invalidating what was lurking inside my emotions, to bring it into the light and to let God's supernatural peace guard my heart and mind in Christ Jesus.

I saw so clearly that if you are out of touch with your emotions like I was, it pays to dig a little bit and find out what's there. If you can't break your system and put it back together again, then you don't really know what your system is. Now I'm a proponent of, "If it ain't broke, break it." Then let God put you back together the right way and show you how your body, soul, and spirit work together by faith, through peace, in the middle of your mess.

CHAPTER 8
OUT OF THE PANIC ROOM

Penny and I instinctively ran into our own separate panic rooms to try to escape the mess my panic attacks were causing. The problem is, once you're in the panic room, you're locked in there all by yourself. It's a dead end. Life doesn't happen alone, hiding out from the pain. The thing that keeps us out of the panic room is community.

I'm fascinated that even in the beginning, when Adam was with God in a perfect garden, it wasn't enough.

And the LORD God said, "It is not good that man should be alone; I will make him a helper comparable to him." —Genesis 2:18 (NKJV)

Imagine that—Adam needed something more than God! He needed someone similar to him. God created the first human community when He created Eve.

The enemy's plan ever since has been to push individuals into isolation, into panic rooms where they are weak and vulnerable. Have you noticed in our culture that people are more isolated now even though we seem to "connect" more? So much of our interaction is artificial, temporary, and shallow—whether online, at work, or in a public place. It's no wonder people are growing lonelier even as social-media relationships increase.

Even Christian culture sometimes pushes the idea that all we need is God. Worship songs talk about being satisfied with Him alone, when the truth is we need God, some solid friends, and our husband or wife if we're married. Otherwise God would have looked on Adam alone and said, "This is really good. He's got me. That's enough."

Proverbs 18:1 (NKJV) makes it really clear: "A man who isolates himself seeks his own desire; He rages against all wise judgment." Notice that people put themselves in panic rooms of isolation because of their own desire (perhaps the desire not to be "shamed" by their imperfections). After enough time in isolation, a person actually becomes angry and violent toward wisdom! A form of insanity sets in.

Isolation is dangerous. Isolation is lonely. Isolation leads to death and destruction.

THE DRAW OF ISOLATION

Isolation is also attractive.

People run into their panic rooms and put themselves in solitary confinement because it's more comfortable to hide the problems and imperfect spots they don't want others to be aware of or get involved with. I flatly did not want anyone to know I was having anxiety issues—especially those who saw me as the strong leader. I didn't want anyone to see me as weak. I wondered what everyone would think of me. So I hid behind my phone, my cheery text messages, my social-media posts. All the while, I was walking through my darkest hour of anxiety and self-doubt.

Panic rooms are attractive because they give us a sense of control over our reputations. We think that by hiding we can actually control what other people think of us. Each of us creates a false self that we present to the world for its approval. The tragedy is that I had always considered myself an open and honest person and enjoyed living that way. Panic attacks stole that openness from me. I began to hide. I preferred the pain of loneliness to the pain of exposure and possible ridicule or disapproval.

The problem is that isolation always leads to hopelessness. Elijah told God, "Take my life. I want this over with." In his own way, he was raging against the wise judgment of which the Proverb speaks. I actually believe that isolation is a spirit, not just a choice we make. It is a spiritual attack of the enemy designed to corner us in a place where he can discourage us and bring shame and guilt such that we seek to end our lives.

This "isolation suicide" takes different forms. Sometimes it's literal. Sometimes it's relational. When people don't know the real you, isn't that a type of invisible death? So many people don't have real relationships but just pantomimes of reality.

Some turn to the slow suicide of drinking as a form of self-medication. "It's just one glass," they say. Then it's four. Then it's a bottle before bed.

Others turn to unhealthy relationships with someone not their spouse. "It's all right. We're just texting. It was just one picture." Good judgment fails by degrees in the panic room.

Being alone becomes easier the more you do it. Presenting a facade of yourself becomes instinctive. The panic room keeps you safe, but from the wrong things. It keeps you from listening to the hard questions, wise advice, and pointed ob-servations of those around you.

I was visiting a pastor friend in another state and preach-ing at his church. This couple's son had been struggling, but they didn't know why. I have a sort of sixth sense for when someone's doing drugs because I grew up around drugs and saw how people behaved. (Penny has a sixth sense about sex-ual sin.) I could tell right away that their son was on drugs, and over dinner with the couple, after listening to them worry about what was wrong, I told them directly, "Your son's doing drugs."

Their reaction surprised me.

"No, he's not," they said. "He's just going through depression."

They didn't even think drug use was in the realm of pos-sibility with their son. I didn't press the point but said, "Go home and test him."

They did and found out he was on drugs, and the problem was a lot more serious than anticipated. Somehow they had gotten themselves into a place of not hearing sound judgment from those around them and had blinded themselves to an obvious fact. This is easier to do when other aspects of your life are going well. Your church or business is growing, your other children are successful, you have ample money and a nice-looking house. We use positives to cover our negatives. All of it is a manifestation of the panic room.

LEARNING TO TRUST

For me, it was easier to cut off true relationships because of a fear of scrutiny, betrayal, and even the work required to maintain them. I felt like the guy Jesus met one day whose friends were carrying him on a mat (Mark 2:1-12). So many times I sympathized with that man, feeling paralyzed, ineffective, immobilized, unresponsive, unproductive, powerless, and restrained. Yet what captures my imagination is how much trust this man possessed to allow others to carry him. What if they dropped him? Wouldn't you be wondering that while they were trucking you through the busy streets? Life was surely safer at home lying on the floor, even if he wouldn't receive a miracle that day.

In my fraternity, in the business world and even in ministry, many people only wanted relationships with me because they wanted something from me. Most people look at you and think about how your talent can help fulfill their vision. I don't think people do this intentionally. Let's be honest for a second; we all have a selfish nature. Few and far between are the people who want something for—not from—you. That caused barriers to go up in my soul. Nobody likes being used or disappointed time and again.

So it's hard to let people carry you, even when you're paralyzed by some problem—sin, panic attacks, personal weakness, or addiction. You may have your own reasons for distrust. In the case of the paralyzed man, he not only allowed his friends to pick him up and carry him, but he allowed them to do something very risky and lower him through the roof of a house. That is a deep level of relationship, or at least desperation! Trust meant being totally vulnerable.

During the years I was having panic attacks, I probably appeared to have more friends and acquaintances than ever before. I just wasn't transparent with them. Most of my true friends lived out of town, and we only connected by phone a few times a year. Even in deeper relationships I didn't open up with people. I was trying to fight my own battles in private.

In our "mat moments" we have to risk being dropped to enjoy the benefits of being carried. It helped me to see that all relationships begin by trusting in God. Proverbs 3:5-6 (NKJV) says to "Trust in the LORD with all your heart, And lean not on your own understanding; In all your ways acknowledge Him, And He shall direct your paths." When we trust God with our relationships, He guides us to the people we need in our lives.

I'm convinced of what author Gary Smalley said: "Life is relationships. The rest is just details." Community creates "with you" moments when we realize that someone very close to us is in the same mess we are in. We look at each other's lives and say, "How do you have a marriage where you dealt with and overcame that problem? Help me get through this."

Miracles happen in community because we are willing to be fully ourselves with other people who are very different from us. It happened for the paralyzed man whose risk paid off. He got his life back that day and had his sins forgiven. Not a bad outcome for letting people carry you!

STAYING IN RELATIONSHIP

I often imagine what the relationship between the disciples Peter and John was like. In my opinion, they were the world's most unlikely ministry pair. John seemed on an emotional

OUT OF THE PANIC ROOM

roller coaster all the time, hot-headed in one moment and sensitive and loving in the next. He wrote about himself as the one whom Jesus loved, who laid his head on His chest at the Last Supper. Peter was the impulsive, cussing, extroverted, physically built and in-your-face fisherman. How easy—or rather hard—was it for these two to be friends with a deep relationship? Can't you picture them competing and fighting all the time? The gospels depict exactly this kind of relationship.

Yet one day they were walking to the temple and met a lame man who was 40 years old (Acts 3:1-10). They recognized the divine nature of this encounter, and when Peter commanded him, the man leapt to his feet. If it hadn't been for their choice to remain in community together, I'm convinced that this kind of ministry moment would not have happened.

Again, deep friendships lead to miraculous results.

Everybody's purpose is intertwined with other people's purposes—yours, mine, all those around us. Our eternities are wrapped up together. Community gives a sense of belonging, but it's ultimately about much more than that. It's about finding our identities in God. Community helps us discover who God is and who we are. The clearer we see Him, the clearer we see ourselves. That is the Christian journey. The essence of what community does, even with its imperfections and difficulties, is to reveal who we are and to point us to Jesus, our Redeemer. This doesn't happen in the panic room. It happens in the presence of true friends who know us deeply and push us to fulfill our highest callings.

We have a phrase at Freedom House: "We belong, we believe, we behave." The order is significant. In most religious and legalistic environments you have to believe and behave like everyone before you belong with them. By contrast, we want people to feel that they belong before they believe and behave like we do. If you feel you belong, I can help you with your beliefs. If you're connected to a community, you'll be open through relationship to change your behavior. One of our deepest human needs is to feel like we belong. When that happens, our hearts are open to hear about a belief change. Behavior always follows belief. If you can change belief, you can change behavior.

Maybe while reading this you realize you are in a panic room of your own making. Why you are there is less important right now than making a decision to get out. The best way to get out of the panic room is to let someone know what's going on with you. Come out of hiding. Make a phone call. Talk to a friend. Visit a counselor or a life coach—someone to walk with you through the whys and the hows. Sometimes it's just a matter of someone sitting with you long enough to let a bad moment pass. Other times it's an invitation to a longer journey.

Get people into your world who are honest with you, who can knock sense into your head. A counselor is good, but remember that counselors are paid to listen to you; they might not be as rough and tumble as someone with skin in the game, someone in your close community whose life is impacted by your decisions. You need friends who will say, "What the heck are you thinking?" Friends who are not impressed with you. As leaders, this is especially important since the position of leadership attracts people who want our favor and who may butter us up with half-truths. You want people who call it like it is, messy, with no filter: "Boom. Here you go. This is the way it is."

Those people are like gold.

I made a decision that I won't allow myself to go back into the panic room, so I have invited a couple of people into my life who like me enough to say, "Hey, you're ignoring this. This is unhealthy." Some of my friends are pretty harsh with me—and that's just what I want. If you don't have anyone who can tell you no, you're a dangerous person.

I'm surprised by how many people don't have somebody who can call them on their stuff. Don't be one of them. Get into real community with somebody.

The second thing I recommend is having a pastor or leader in a position over you whom you can call or text and wave a white flag to say, "Hey, I'm struggling." Friends can help a lot, and counselors are great, but there is a place for someone with spiritual authority and maturity to speak into our lives, to comfort and encourage us in the unique way that leaders can.

I am convinced that my life, our marriage, and our church are stronger because of what we have gone through—and we continue to get stronger. Coming out of the panic room created a powerful opportunity to pursue our goal of being relationally healthy people in community together.

CHAPTER 9
REST IS A WEAPON

Lack of rest was a big part of what caused things to go wrong for me. I had very little margin or wiggle room in my schedule. I didn't take time to let my mind and body recuperate. It seems obvious now, but I had to learn it in real time. Returning to effectiveness meant I had to learn how to disconnect in a healthy, balanced way.

There is so much pressure on people to succeed, pursue ambitions, do bigger things, do better things, make more money, use their gifts, have the right friends, get the promotions, and accomplish the next big "win." I was no stranger to this. Reflecting on my life as a kid, I recognized the impulse to succeed so I could improve my circumstances. Mom and I were very poor, so at an early age I worked my way into the lifestyle and cash flow I wanted. When I was 12 years old, I already had two newspaper delivery routes. I got up by myself at 4 a.m. and rode my bike around delivering newspapers. At 13, I started working at a dude ranch cutting grass and cooking. By the time I was 15, I was working at numerous restaurants—McDonald's, Bojangles Louisiana-style chicken restaurant, anywhere that took a worker's permit. At 16, I worked at a gas station. At 18, I got a job at a bank. I have held jobs ever since.

When I hear young adults these days say they want four-day workweeks, shorter workdays, family leave, plus four weeks of vacation per year, it's a little hard for me to sympathize. I value hard work, and I think God does, too.

My work ethic carried over into ministry. Penny and I both are very driven. We pushed the church forward with all the enthusiasm and energy we had, and the growth and attention we received seemed to justify the work and sacrifice we poured in. The problem was with my motivation. Far too often I was pushing harder and climbing higher not because I wanted God to get the glory but because I wanted people to approve of me. It validated me and provided more "look what I've accomplished" moments. My inability to rest sprang from a struggle with my own identity. I lacked the confidence to rest and ended up doing stuff for the wrong reasons. Rest seemed a waste of time. When I tried to rest, I kept thinking, *I should be working on something, writing a message, planning our next event.* I was focused on justifying my existence, proving my success.

It's a terrible way to live. It can be productive in the short term, but it's not fulfilling in any lasting way.

When you're tired and over-worked in ministry, you fall into the trap of what Craig Groeschel calls being a full-time minister and a part-time Christian. Instead of spending time with the Lord and enjoying His presence and Word for personal reflection, you tend to look at everything as fodder for your next message. Your whole life is built around performing well on the weekends (and any other time you speak to people) by giving a good sermon or talk. Someone said it's like having a baby every Sunday and getting pregnant every Monday. You give birth every seven days to a new message and then have to come up with something fresh again the following week. It can be a grind. Your personal time with God—and with your wife and family—suffers as work and performance take center stage.

DISCOVERING REST

The Bible clearly values rest more than a lot of us do.

Therefore, since a promise remains of entering His rest, let us fear lest any of you seem to have come short of it. —Hebrews 4:1 (NKJV)

This passage always intrigued me—and bothered me. What did it mean that a promise of rest remains? Why did God rest after six days of creation? I didn't dig into these questions until panic attacks forced me to define my ideas about rest in a very practical way, and I've come to the following conclusions:

- Rest is not a weakness. Rest is a weapon.

- Rest is a powerful force. It is something God Himself did. Who are we to think that we don't need it?

- Rest is productive. It refreshes the mind and percolates new ideas. Rest is also when our physical muscles grow and rebuild after working out or simply living.

- Rest helps our brains recover and can save us from making bad decisions.

- Rest provides the best recovery for our emotions and souls.

- Rest happens when we are confident in our identity and

purpose. When you are strong in who God says you are, you can take a break knowing that you will be better on the other side.

You are no longer the slave of the approval addict inside of you.

In my life, there had to come a point where the pain of what I was going through actually caused me to change. It was like God saying, "If you're not going to take a rest, I'll make you take one." Learning how to turn off was a big learning curve for me. I remember seeing Andy Stanley's book *Choosing to Cheat,* which is about letting things go that you are not responsible for. The title alone unlocked healthy behavior for me. I knew I had to invest in long-term values, prioritize things that were in my control and ability to do, and start saying no to everything else. One of the hardest lessons to learn was that for every "yes" there has to be a "no" somewhere.

In practical terms, you have to set a day of rest and guard it like a pit bull. Resting is not something you accidentally do. It doesn't happen on the run. It is a planned, intentional activity of the utmost importance. I am intentional and even strict with my staff about it. I told them, "This is my day off. I don't want you to call me unless someone who is close to me is dying, or the building is burning down."

Then I had to guard my schedule from its worst enemy: me. I'm like every other person. It's easy for my mind to start processing what happened on Sunday, or other ministry-related stuff, or what is ahead on my calendar. I had to train myself to say, "Nope, not gonna do that." For me, that meant coming to a point where I just didn't care. I think you know what I mean. To truly disconnect mentally and emotionally from my role as Pastor Troy, I had to make rest more important than anything else in that moment. It wasn't (and isn't) easy. It takes practice and discipline. But I like it.

I established Monday as my day off. I spend time with Penny. We have breakfast together, go to lunch together, watch our shows together, or just sit and be together. We enjoy our home as a place of peace and rest.

THE VALUE OF FUN

I also had to find out what activities helped me rest and recover and find hobbies that energized me mentally and physically. I had downplayed these aspects of life for too long. I met the Lord in a movement in which everything is dealt with spiritually. Every solution is to read the Bible every day and pray. But God has a broader approach: He wants us physically, emotionally, and mentally healthy, and those areas of life require our attention, too. Not everything is strictly spiritual. It's like the person who is 75 pounds overweight and has bad knees and diabetes. Can God heal that person instantly? Of course. But does He want that person to develop discipline, gain victory and treat his body like a temple, so that other problems go away? Absolutely, He does.

For me, "fun" looked like playing golf, spending time with close friends, watching movies, and working out. I remember getting the Groupon for CrossFit and falling in love with it. I liked the competition, the community, and the opportunity to connect with non-believers in a safe environment. I have been able to minister to people who don't even think about church and show them that Christians can be normal, competitive, fun, active people. I happen to think that the church can learn a lot from how CrossFit builds successful, close communities.

Paul wrote in 1 Corinthians 6:19 (NKJV) "Do you not know that your body is the temple of the Holy Spirit who is in you, whom you have from God, and you are not your own?" I have really taken that to heart and continue to reap the benefits. We also have a small home gym (and just added an assault bike, a crazy piece of equipment). If I can't go to the gym one day, I wake up and work out for twenty or thirty minutes. There's no excuse.

All of this qualifies as rest, as I get my mind outside the routine of normal responsibility.

HIS BRIDE, NOT MINE

On the spiritual side, I had to learn to distinguish between studying for a message and getting to know God simply for my own good. I am still learning. I read my Bible daily and am careful not to let it become a mindless habit. I'm naturally a morning guy, and having devotions is the first thing I do. Within that time, I change things up to keep it new and interesting. There are seasons when I pray more, and some when I study Scripture more. I like to read through and spend time in the New Testament and other books. Sometimes I read off my iPad. Sometimes I switch to a paper Bible to make things different. I will change the translation for a season to mix it up a little bit. It's like applying the exercise principle of muscle confusion to keep my spirit and soul engaged and strong.

I also try to read a chapter a day in a spiritual book. I listen to messages from other preachers on podcasts and seek out new voices. In all of this, I'm spending time listening to God's voice, being cognizant of His conviction. Discipleship is not four classes and a certificate; it's a lifelong journey. The Bible says,

This Book of the Law shall not depart from your mouth, but you shall meditate in it day and night, that you may observe to do according to all that is written in it. For then you will make your way prosperous, and then you will have good success. —*Joshua 1:8 (NKJV)*

That's what I want—to have good success, on God's terms.

One of the phrases I heard that helped me most was spoken by T. D. Jakes: "It's not my job to love God's bride. It's my job to feed God's bride and love mine." I had been taking responsibility for the church that wasn't my responsibility. I treated it like it was my deal, and it wasn't my deal. I took credit or blame for its growth or level of engagement. I think it was Rick Warren who said, "It's not our job to build the church; it's our job to build people." To be a ministry leader means maintaining a level of trust in God that it is not my church or Penny's church or our church—it is God's church. Sometimes we think our mistakes or failures can mess the whole thing up. But as I heard one man say, "The anointing is not that fragile." If we make ourselves too big in the equation, then we are basically saying we are God. We have mentally taken ownership of His bride, which is a scary and overwhelming proposition.

I have concluded that we may at times disappoint the Holy Spirit and disappoint people, but we can't stop His work as much as we think we can. The Holy Spirit is not like a glass jar you drop off the table, and it shatters. His work is durable and outlasts our failures. It is His church, not ours. It's okay with me if "my" church is not growing as fast as every other church around. Growth is His concern. Mine is staying healthy and growing healthy people.

What surprised me was that while we were walking through my panic attacks and learning to live healthier, Freedom House continued growing, maturing, and gaining as much ground as ever. It was almost like my overwork had nothing to do with it. I wish I'd known that when I started the thing! But, better late than never. I had to mature to a place of appreciating that Freedom House's health and growth were always more about God than my efforts. After all, Jesus said, "I will build My church" (Matthew 16:18, NKJV). That's exactly what He was doing, maybe even in spite of what I was going through.

Valuing rest was so healthy for me and Penny personally that we implemented plans for our staff to prioritize rest, too. We encourage our leaders to take time off and disconnect from responsibilities. We live by, "Every seven days a Sabbath. Every seven weeks a Sunday off. Every seven months a vacation." We instituted a policy with our staff pastors that every seven years they receive a four-week paid sabbatical.

There are still seasons when we have to push hard, but they are within a larger context that values rest and the faith it requires to say, "I'm taking a day off every week, and I know God will continue to accomplish what He wants in my job and through my ministry."

CHAPTER 10
I'M NOT ALONE

Penny and I and our kids were heading to one of our favorite events of the year, a get-away gathering with a few hundred other ministry families from around the nation. The meetings, held on an invitation-only basis on the weekend after Father's Day, were always held in a nice hotel, and we spent time around the pool getting to know other church leaders and pastors, playing in a golf tournament, and having meals together. A lot of well-known Christian leaders attended, but the vibe remained very laid-back. There was no greenroom. Nobody was pushing their ministry agenda or comparing their numbers and influence against anyone else's. It was about helping ministry families get refreshed and build relationships with people we normally wouldn't get to spend time with in a casual environment.

Every year, the morning and evening meetings were relaxed and meaningful as we enjoyed panels or featured speakers who brought messages aimed at the realities of being in ministry. One fun aspect was the seven-on-seven sessions. They picked seven people to speak for seven minutes each. A countdown clock in the back buzzed when each person's seven minutes were up. The format was fast and entertaining and allowed us to hear from different communicators in a short amount of time.

A few days ahead of the gathering, the organizers asked me to participate as a seven-on-seven speaker. I was excited for the invitation and wanted to share something good. As I started working on my message, God surprised me. "I want you to talk about your panic attacks," He said.

"No, I don't want to talk about that," came my first reply. I sometimes forget it's useless to argue with God.

"I want you to talk about what you went through," I felt Him say again. "Be vulnerable in this moment."

"But God, I don't want to be vulnerable," I protested. "All my heroes, people I look up to, are going to be in that room. I want to talk about something fun and exciting, and show off my teaching gift."

I felt the silent, unmistakable pressure to obey, and though inwardly I was groaning, I began to think it through. How would I share my story in seven minutes and give some practical application? Could I condense my thoughts enough to be clear and effective? How would it feel to be so vulnerable in front of so many people I respected? I decided to divide my seven minutes into two parts, focusing on my story for a few minutes, then talking about the power of rest.

Our family was excited to arrive in Scottsdale, Arizona. My kids loved getting to know other pastors' kids who shared similar experiences that few others understood. I always enjoyed playing in the golf tournament and lounging around the pool. Penny enjoyed all the ladies and of course the shopping. I am convinced that if gold medals were given out for shopping, she would stand center podium every time.

The morning of the seven-on-seven session arrived, and Penny and I made our way to the ballroom where the meetings were held.

"Lord, are you sure you want me to talk about this?" I asked one more time. The response was a clear confirmation. "Okay," I said, "but you'd better make it good."

I made my way to the round table up front where the day's speakers were sitting. Prepared notes were in my hand, because there was no way I was going to wing a seven-minute talk in that environment. Still, I was finding it hard to hide my nerves. Adrenaline coursed through my body, causing my mind to race and my hands to tingle.

Here I am, about to talk about panic attacks, and I'm wrestling with one right now! I thought. I could hardly believe the irony and pressure of possibly experiencing a panic attack while speaking about how to avoid one.

Given the nature of the format, my turn came quickly. I gathered my notes and walked forward as people clapped both for me and for the guy who had just concluded. Setting my notes on the podium, I looked out and saw faces most people only see on television or on the covers of books. These guys—by their examples—had helped define my ministry approach. I had gotten to know a number of them personally and considered them friends and great leaders in the church. Now I was going to tell them about the messiest part of my life.

I can't believe I'm doing this, I thought one more time. *Here goes.*

Looking down at my notes, I launched into my story. It flowed more easily than I had expected, and I kept glancing at the clock so I wouldn't run out of time and hear that merciless buzzer. In just a few minutes I was transitioning to three thoughts about the power of rest that I drew from the book of

Hebrews and my own experience. With the seconds ticking down, I made a few final statements and thanked everyone for listening.

I did it—and I beat the buzzer! I thought as I picked up my notes and headed back to the table. *At least it's over.* I barely remembered what I had said, but the applause seemed more amplified than normal. I looked around, and sure enough, those in attendance were on their feet, clapping. They were giving me a standing ovation!

Penny leaned over to me as I sat down beside her.

"You did a great job. That was awesome," she whispered in my ear.

This was an encouraging environment, by design, but the affirmation still felt good. Best of all, I had avoided experiencing a panic attack in one of the most nerve-wracking moments of my life.

But the real surprise came when the meeting ended. People started heading out for lunch, but a number of ministers in attendance, including popular leaders of our day, came directly over to me. One grabbed my elbow.

"I want to talk to you more about what you said," he said. "I've had similar experiences. I'd like to hear your thoughts."

We exchanged phone numbers.

"Thank you for sharing that," said another. "I struggle with the same thing, and I'm on medication for it, too."

One by one, these men—whom I held in such high esteem—and who led millions by their example, confided that they, too, had experienced panic attacks. Over the next few days, many other fellow ministers told me their own stories with panic attacks as well.

I had no idea it was so common! I thought time and again. I never would have guessed that some of these guys walked through the same stuff I did.

And then he told me, "My grace is enough; it's all you need. My strength comes into its own in your weakness." Once I heard that, I was glad to let it happen. I quit focusing on the handicap and began appreciating the gift. It was a case of Christ's strength moving in on my weakness. —2 Corinthians 12:9 (The Message)

This passage was written by the apostle Paul. He wrote two-thirds of the New Testament. Other than Jesus Himself, he was probably the most influential believer in the ancient world. He was describing a weakness. He was describing a crack in life, an area that plagued him. I have read this passage hundreds—if not thousands—of times. He didn't have to write this. He didn't have to show his area of insecurity and shortcoming. But he did! Why? God's grace is attracted to our weakness. It's when we reveal our humanity that God can pour out His power in our lives.

I don't know about you, but I need more of God's grace in my life. When it comes to anxiety and panic attacks, I am weak, but God is strong. I don't know what weakness may be in your life. I would think that if you picked up this book it has something to do with panic attacks or anxiety. I want you to know that God's grace is available to you.

WELCOMING THE HOLY SPIRIT INTO OUR MESSES

The goal is to find God in the middle of our messes. The Holy Spirit actually wants to be invited into the negative stuff we've got going on. The Bible calls Him our Comforter, Advocate, Intercessor, Counselor, Strengthener, the One who walks alongside us and will never leave us. He is eternal and good, our teacher, purifier, guide into all truth, companion in every situation, empowerer, illuminator, standby and helper.

Jesus made it clear that it was best for Him (Jesus) to go away. That is an amazing statement, but when we realize all that the Holy Spirit is and does for us, it makes sense. The reality is that through relationship with the Holy Spirit, we can get to know Jesus even better than if Jesus were with us now in the flesh. It's hard to grasp, but it's true.

Think of it this way. If any of us had been given the opportunity to be on earth when Jesus was, we probably would not have believed in Him. Many in Jesus' day got bored of His ministry, or concluded that His teaching was too difficult, or even that He was a bad person. They did not have the Holy Spirit, because the Holy Spirit had not yet been given. Who's to say you and I wouldn't have joined the crowd who found Jesus' presence too disruptive to our daily lives? But with the Holy Spirit, we experience the reality of Jesus' presence in a far greater and more intimate way. We have Him in a way we couldn't if He were physically present.

Some Christians shy away from relationship with the Holy Spirit, maybe because they feel they're getting along fine without giving Him too much thought, or because they've seen other people taking things to a weird extreme. In doing this, they forfeit the kind of help all of us need in our messy lives.

They remind me of when Penny and I got married. I had a waterbed. It was great for a single guy, but Penny wanted no part of it. She announced right away, "We're getting rid of that thing, and we're getting a real bed." So we bought a big and rather expensive bed in our newlywed zeal.

"Now we need to buy a comforter," Penny said. She's way more sophisticated than I am, so I went along with the idea. I didn't know the difference between a blanket and a comforter, but we went to a few stores and finally found this amazing, warm comforter. Back home, I was fired up. I couldn't wait to get in bed underneath this comforter. But I came into the room that night, and the comforter was folded up in the corner.

"What's going on? Why isn't the comforter on the bed?" I asked.

Penny told me, "The comforter is for looks, not for use."

I couldn't believe I had spent that much money on something we would never actually use! But that is how we treat the Holy Spirit so many times. He is the Comforter we must relate to if we want any effectiveness and peace in our lives. Whatever your mess is, dig into that relationship. Apologize for putting Him off to the side and ask yourself, *What does it look like for the Holy Spirit to be involved in every part of my life? What does it look like for Him to be my Intercessor?* He prays for us when we don't know how to pray. How can He be your Counselor? He gives wisdom necessary to navigate every challenge. Your Strengthener? When you are going through problems and feel too anxious to do anything, He strengthens you. Your standby? He is there to bail you out when you find yourself in a fix.

My goal is not just to share my journey with you, so we can sympathize with each other. I want to point all of us to a deeper relationship with the Holy Spirit. Your mess can be an open door to a richer relationship with God than you ever knew was possible, even as a Christian. There is so much more of Him to know, to experience, to draw from, and it begins by saying "yes" to a greater presence and work of the Holy Spirit in our lives.

Let's end this book where every lasting solution starts: in prayer.

Holy Spirit, I invite you into my situation. Come, be all of Who you are in my life and in my mess. I believe you have the answers I need, and I look forward to knowing you better as we walk through stuff together. I say "yes" to taking this journey with you. In Jesus' name, Amen!